Client Praise

Quanta Change is the first technique I've used that has provided lasting, positive results. After six months, not only am I seeing positive results, I continue to improve. My emotional hills and valleys are evening out, which means I have more energy to accomplish what I want and overcome issues that were overwhelming me half a year ago. So glad I discovered it.

—Betty

Quanta Change helped me work through my patterns of taking on responsibility for others' behaviors, to the point of even apologizing for it or trying to fix other peoples' actions. Sara helped me deconstruct and change these patterns. It's an enlightening and empowering process. Sara's work is a guiding light to lead you through and emerge on the other side happier and more peaceful, with feelings of competence and well-being.

—Ann Marie

Sara Avery, with the tool of Quanta Change, made a lasting, positive impact on my life. The process gave me a broader way to understand myself, my challenges, and my habits. Quanta Change quiets the pain and fear inherent in the human condition and taps into a sense of wellness and confidence to address life without overwhelming or paralyzing anxiety.

—Carmen

Many close personal and work relationships were difficult and felt like I was always living in a world of chaos. Today, I feel much calmer and these relationships flow much easier than ever before—the difference is amazing! Sara's knowledge and guidance have made all the difference and I'm so grateful for finding this process. I highly recommend Quanta Change and honestly can't wait to see what else I learn on this journey of relying on my well-being.

—Suzanne

Since finding this work and taking it seriously, I have seen generational chains of depression and misery fall away from my life—no exaggeration. I am deeply grateful for Mimi Herrmann and Sara Avery's grounded research and dedication to helping humanity rise from its individual (and therefore collective) Learned Distress. This book is a clear and easy explanation for how what seemed impossible became reality for me.

—Ellie

I became aware of Quanta Change in the early 2000s and worked with both Mimi Hermann and Sara Avery. During the time they were my guides, I had what turned into a wonderful experience traveling with both my sisters in Italy. Generally, being with my older sister was a challenge, but during this trip, I was able to step back and see her for who she is as I enjoyed myself for who I am! I am very grateful for that enormous shift.

—Mollie

I came into Quanta Change having reached what was seemingly a dead end of my process of self-transformation into who I believed I am, how I was *supposed* to do things, and what I was meant to be. Quanta Change has really helped in learning the true causes of my own roadblocks, fear, failures, and general way of moving through the world. Despite the sometimes-uncomfortable processes of Learned Distress being burned away, I find myself able to better identify and navigate situations that would have frozen and frustrated me prior to my Quanta Change journey. I encourage anyone looking for real change within themselves to give Quanta Change a try.

—B.L.

I have struggled since childhood relating to others and had topped out with traditional therapy when I began my Quanta Change journey with Sara. Quanta Change has helped me to understand my feelings with more clarity and has allowed me to feel comfortable in personal relationships that I had previously struggled with.

—Renee

With Quanta Change, I've had so many "aha" moments that it blows my mind. I've finally found a person and a process that understands the core of my unease, and this is after a 40-year journey of self-discovery. I've tried everything from meditation to acupuncture, hypnotherapy, exercise, diet changes, chiropractic treatments, medicine, and counseling. But I continued to feel the same: "Why don't I feel right inside?" I found myself 40 years old, having conquered all financial and business goals, blessed with a loving wife and four beautiful children, but still that unease remained. Quanta Change has helped me unpeel all my protective layers built over time, to help uncover my truth, my happiness. Quanta Change gives me hope that I can finally be me!

—Mac

When I first began Quanta Change, I was able to cognitively recognize that I had unhealthy behavioral patterns in my interpersonal relationships (specifically, romantic partnerships), but I could not change my deep feeling of fear that no matter what I did, romantic relationships would always seem to end in heartache for me. When I began Quanta Change, I always felt like I couldn't say no. I felt I had to do whatever my partner wanted in order to maintain the relationship. Now, I feel confident that I can say "no" or "not right now" or "I need time to think about what you're asking of me." My fear was always if I don't say yes, my partner would get upset or they'd leave. But now when I actually do say no, people respect my decision. I can now be comfortable saying what I really feel in a way that's respectful to both myself and others. Decades of cognitive behavioral therapy cannot do what Sara Avery and I have been able to do. I highly recommend her services to anyone who wants to make lasting changes in their life and feel better about who they are on the inside.

—Tamara

FEEL GOOD BEING YOU

OVERCOME YOUR ROADBLOCKS TO
DEEP, LASTING CHANGE

SARA AVERY

Modern Wisdom
PRESS

Modern Wisdom Press
Boulder, Colorado, USA
www.modernwisdompress.com

Copyright © Sara Avery, 2021
Quanta Change®, Learned Distress®, and Sensory Quotient® used by permission of Sara Avery.

All rights reserved. No part of this book may be reproduced in any form without permission in writing from the author. Reviewers may quote brief passages in reviews.

Published 2020

Cover Design: Karen Sperry Design
Author's photo courtesy of ELC Photography

DISCLAIMER

No part of this publication may be reproduced or transmitted in any form or by any means, mechanical or electronic, including photocopying or recording, or by any information storage and retrieval system, or transmitted by email, without permission in writing from the author.

Neither the author nor the publisher assumes any responsibility for errors, omissions, or contrary interpretations of the subject matter within.

MEDICAL DISCLAIMER

The information in this book is a result of years of practical experience by the author. This information is not intended as a substitute for the advice provided by your physician or other healthcare professional. Do not use the information in this book for diagnosing or treating a health problem or disease, or prescribing medication or other treatment.

For Mimi,
whose heart for humanity and
brilliance have enabled us to
uncover our own well-being.
I will never forget
your generosity, love, and
kindness.

CONTENTS

Introduction *1*

Chapter 1	Why Is It So Hard to Feel Good Just Being You?	5
Chapter 2	Why Do Negative Situations and Patterns Keep Happening Despite Your Very Best Efforts to Stop Them?	23
Chapter 3	How Is Sleep Perpetuating Your Negative Patterns?	39
Chapter 4	Why Hasn't Everything You've Tried to Feel Better Worked?	45
Chapter 5	How Can Sleep Be at the Heart of the Solution to Your Biggest Problems?	51
Chapter 6	Change During Sleep—Really? Could It Actually Work for Me?	59
Chapter 7	The Quanta Change Sensory Quotient (SQ)	67
Chapter 8	The Idealist SQ Pattern	75
Chapter 9	The Defeatist SQ Pattern	83
Chapter 10	The Perfectionist SQ Pattern	89
Chapter 11	The Optimist SQ Pattern	95
Chapter 12	The Caregiver SQ Pattern	101
Chapter 13	The (Benevolent) Dictator Pattern	109
Chapter 14	How to Overcome Common Obstacles and Bumps on Your Quanta Change Path	115
Chapter 15	Conclusion: It's Time for You to Feel Good Just Being Yourself!	127

About The Author: Sara Avery *131*
Acknowledgments *132*
Thank You *134*

Introduction

Sixteen years ago, I ran into a friend I hadn't seen in a few years. We exchanged the usual greetings but instead of moving on when I replied that I was doing well, she looked concerned. "But Sara, how is your health?" I instantly felt embarrassed for her because she clearly had me confused with someone else. And then I realized that I was the confused one. She was remembering quite accurately that the last time we were together my long struggle to solve my endocrine system issues was at the center of my life.

So, how had I forgotten something that had been so important? What enabled my ability to forget such a huge, personal battle is the reason I'm writing this book. That amnesia was accompanied by profound, positive change in every part of my life. I felt so much better in so many ways that I knew I had to help other people experience the same kind of change, and so I made Quanta Change® my life's work.

Quanta Change removes layers of the feeling that you absorbed early in life that there's something wrong with you being just who you are. This feeling, called Learned Distress®, not only feels awful, but it is the automatic generating force for the negative situations in your life—in your relationships, work life, health, daily life, and how you express yourself. And Learned Distress does this despite all of your (probably exhaustive!) attempts to feel better and make your life work better.

There are many "flavors" of Learned Distress, like "I don't matter," "I always have to be perfect," "I always have to win," "I need everyone to like me," and "I can't achieve what matters to me," to name a few. And then those feelings keep generating situations and negative patterns in which you feel those same ways, which can include struggling to feel better or have things go well in various parts of your life.

For instance, you might keep finding yourself in abusive relationships despite your very best efforts to find someone who will treat you better. Maybe you do everything right in your education and career development but keep feeling held back. You might struggle to be healthy. Or you just keep procrastinating when it comes to all the things you know you should be doing—this is one I hear a lot!

What I offer you in this book is not another way to overcome adversity. It's not just another way to cope with your difficult feelings and situations. It's not a way to reframe them or find gratitude in spite of them. It's a way to remove the source of your negative feelings and situations. When you do that, the natural well-being at your core gets freed up to become the generating force behind more and more of your life.

So what does that look and feel like? You might not feel the same anxiety getting ready for a big presentation anymore and it goes even better than ever. Or you might not worry about something

Introduction

that you have spent every day of your life worrying about, like what people think about you or whether you did something correctly, or—if you're like lots of people—well, everything! You might start taking better care of yourself without the Herculean effort that was required in the past. You might be able to relax and be yourself around others in a way you've never experienced.

You might find that people are actually hearing you and treating you better than before without you doing or saying anything differently. You might feel a new, underlying hope for your future.

These are the kinds of experiences that I hear about from my clients every day, and they are the experiences I can't wait to help you experience.

CHAPTER 1

Why Is It So Hard to Feel Good Just Being You?

If you're reading this book, you've probably been trying for a long time to feel good, maybe decades, and nothing you have tried has worked for long—if at all. Maybe the struggle is in one part of your life, like your relationships, your health, your work life, your daily habits, or how you express yourself in the world. Maybe all of the above? Or perhaps you just don't feel good *being you.*

You might have spent a lot of time and money trying to feel better, and in that process, you've dug deeply into the reasons you feel awful. If so, you probably have some idea of where it's coming from and might have traced it back to childhood. And yet you feel like you're spinning your wheels. Knowing *why* you feel bad and where it came from hasn't helped you feel any better.

You might even know how you're *supposed* to feel. You might say, "I've learned that I don't need to make everyone happy," or "I just need to clean up all this clutter like the book said and then I'll feel better." And yet you wake up every day feeling the pressure to make everyone happy. Or you just *added* to the clutter today, instead of clearing it out. Or while you support everyone you love to stand up for themselves and be themselves, something holds you back from doing that for yourself, tells you that's not okay for you, or maybe you even feel like it's not *safe* to do that.

I struggled with this, too. Nearly 20 years ago, I was sitting on a blanket in a Colorado mountain meadow listening to a new friend tell me about how his life had changed when he was a subject in a research project. He said that he took a personality test, slept with a recording playing at night, and talked to the researcher every week. He said that this work had gotten rid of the blocks that prevented him from getting into a doctoral program, among other things. In fact, he was thriving in school in ways that catered to his uniqueness, and he largely credited that to being part of this research project.

While listening to what felt wrong in my life emotionally, health-wise, and in my career, he suggested that it could help me to feel better, too. I don't remember my exact response, but it was something like, "Um . . . play a recording while you sleep, and talk to some lady, and my life is going to change?! Yeah, right." He kept insisting for a couple of months, and because he wouldn't let it go, and I really liked spending time with him and his awesome wolf-dogs (and being a dog person, dog people often hold a lot of sway with me), I thought, "Why not? What could it hurt to find out a little bit more?"

I soon learned from the researcher he spoke of that the feeling that something is wrong with me was actually the source of all my problems. And I started playing that recording at night and talking to her regularly, and my life did actually start to change in ways I'd never imagined were possible. Fast forward a couple of decades to today, and not only is every part of my life so much better, but I've been able to help so many others have that same kind of unprecedented improvement in their lives through my work as a Quanta Change Guide.

You're Not Alone

You might believe your way of feeling bad is unique to you, but I assure you that's far from the truth. First, feeling awful always boils down to the feeling that there's something wrong with you being just who you are, which is called Learned Distress. And then, what I have seen over the past two decades is that there are some common forms of Learned Distress that you share with most people. I want to throw a few of them out here to give you a sense of what I mean.

First, the most fundamental pain everyone shares is the feeling that you don't matter just for being yourself. One client said she felt like she'd been walking around her whole life with a sign on her back that read "kick me." Another client said that no one ever respected her wishes, so she kept more assertively setting boundaries, and yet people kept ignoring that and continuing to overstep her comfort zone. And I could write a whole book of anecdotes similar to the time a client said, "I have done absolutely everything people want from me, and yet they never listen to me or give what I am asking from them."

On another front, you may have to work really hard to be healthy or you struggle to stay healthy, like my client, a teacher who got sick and lost her voice several times each school year. This goes for your mental and emotional health, too. You might often feel depressed, angry, or anxious, like a client that went into every meeting feeling on the edge of panic, despite a long professional history of success.

Maybe you feel that you always have to be perfect. One of my clients was at the top of her field with a couple of decades of accomplishments, awards, and accolades, and yet she still suffered from imposter syndrome, fearing that her next presentation would be the moment when everyone would see that she was the fraud she feared herself to be. She realized that nothing in her decades of education and hard work enabled her to get rid of that underlying feeling that she needed to be more perfect and never could be.

Perhaps you worry a lot about what other people think about you or you feel constant pressure to get their approval or fit in with them. Maybe you even lose sleep over it, like I often used to. One of my clients said, "I don't even know what *I* want or need. I just know that I always *must* keep everyone around me happy."

You might find it difficult to get stuff done. Maybe it's just small, daily tasks, and you procrastinate even with things that should be easy to finish. (Confession: My biggest one is pulling weeds!) Or maybe you really struggle with bigger goals, like my client who just couldn't meet her work deadlines, even though her tasks weren't difficult, and she was running an increasingly high risk of being fired.

You might keep wondering why feeling good has to be *so hard*. One client said, "My marriage and friendships are great, I'm healthy, and I have a good job, and yet none of that has made me feel as good as I thought it would. I'm starting to wonder if something is really wrong with me because I don't know what else I could have done, and I should be happier than I am right now."

Perhaps someone has asked you—or you've asked yourself—why you *choose* to feel bad. Well, let me say emphatically that none of this is your fault, and *no one* chooses to feel bad or have things go wrong in their life. One of the reasons I wrote this book is to explain why you struggle with feeling bad and show you that no matter how differently we all feel lousy, what we have in common is the frustration of trying to change that.

There's something else I want to make clear. Nothing I say in this book negates the fact that other people's bad behavior, whether on an individual, societal, or systemic level, can have an immense negative impact on you. There is no victim-blaming here, and others are always fully responsible for their own bad behavior toward you—full stop.

Having said that, what I have seen over and over is that how you feel about being yourself can increase the potential that you are on the receiving end of the negative ways someone is capable of behaving. Especially if you see a negative pattern in relationships—for instance, you're always ignored or you always have to do more than your share—that points to the likelihood that your Learned Distress plays a role and, therefore, you have the power to change your side of that equation. The personal change I'll lay out for you in this book has the potential to give you more access to your internal support resources to deal with difficult people and bigger world situations that impact you, and also a smoother path for you with those difficult people or systemic challenges.

The Research and Development of Quanta Change

This work is based on several decades of research led by Quanta Change founder and principal researcher Mimi Herrmann. You'll find an overview of it here and then be introduced to specific pieces of the research as we go along. Herrmann had degrees in psychology and education, followed by a long career in health care administration that included work in stress management and substance-use disorder treatment. Her expertise was recognized in 1991 when she was invited to and joined the U.S. National Institutes of Health committee that established the Office of Alternative Medicine (now the National Center for Complementary and Alternative Medicine). She observed and became frustrated that each of these fields—psychology, education, and healthcare—were only treating symptoms and not getting to the source of the problems they treated. She embarked on over a decade of formal research to look for the source of non-well-being, eventually discovering that source, which she named Learned Distress, as well as finding a way to address it: the Quanta Change Process.

Phase One of three in her formal research was part of a Humana Heart Foundation study on recidivism in heart disease, in which she first identified Learned Distress. This is when she also developed the Quanta Change Sensory Quotient® (SQ) personality tool with analysis by a statistician of the hundreds of research participants' data input. The SQ is a personality test that, when graphed, shows us a picture of your Learned Distress and the way you survive with it. (I'll give you a link at the end of the book to take the test and get your own SQ report so you can see it for yourself.) Herrmann presented this original research at a World Health Organization conference in Singapore.

Phase Two, which Herrmann conducted in collaboration with Patrick McGraw, PhD, professor of neurophysiology at the University of Louisville, focused on how the brain develops and how human development is determined by laws of physics. The third phase at Herrmann's Quanta Center for Learning and Development, which included continued input from Dr. McGraw and the input from hundreds more research participants, saw the development of the Quanta Change Process itself.

This development continued through the five-year collaboration in which Herrmann and I further refined the process, and I began guiding people through the process as I have continued to do so. Mimi Herrmann passed away in 2007 and I have continued to develop and refine the work she began. I have made it my life's vocation to make sure it can help many more people feel better.

How Did You Get Your Learned Distress in the First Place?

Maybe you read the question above and thought, "Sara, I've done 20 years of therapy. I'm tired of considering where this stuff came from. I just want to feel better!" I totally get you. But bear with me. Understanding exactly how you got here is really going to help you feel better in the long run, I promise!

A Teensy Tiny Bit of Science

To explain, I'm going to get into a bit of basic physics here. If science is not your thing, don't worry! I'll keep this simple, and I'll give you examples along the way to help you grasp the underpinnings of Quanta Change.

The first bit of science, which was discovered in Phase Two of Herrmann's research, explains why Quanta Change is named that. Physicists define the term "quanta" as a discreet packet or bundle of energy particles. Any *thing* is a quanta—a rock, a phone, a flower.

The energy particles that make up that quanta behave according to the laws that physicists have discovered over the past few hundred years.

Think about it. We human beings are things that are made up of energy particles, just like any other quanta. Therefore, our energy particles must have to obey those same physics laws, right? So, what does that mean?

Normally, when we think about how our lives unfold, we think about our human behavior—how we choose or decide to act and the consequences of those actions. But Quanta Change makes a fundamental distinction about how our lives work. Instead of looking at our rational, human behavior, Quanta Change sees our lives as the *automatic* behavior of human energy—beyond our rational input or control.

I know the idea of a force beyond your rational control somehow affecting your life could be a bit anxiety-producing. If so, stop reading, and take a few deep breaths.

Okay, so, the reality is that even if you feel like you've been in control of your life, like it's been the result of a series of rational choices and decisions, the underlying force driving things has been this automatic behavior of energy. I'm here to help you understand how that has worked and put it to work for you, so you can feel good and have your life function more easily.

Your Starting Point is Chaos—No, Really!

The first law is from the chaos scientists who worked starting in the 1960s to discover how systems develop and work. In scientific terms, chaos actually means the subtle order within a seemingly random system, so it's not as scary as it sounds. Although, perhaps you're thinking, "Chaos sounds like a perfect way to describe my life right now!" This law describes how you become your unique human self.

The chaos scientists' law says that the energy particles that make up a quanta are sensitively dependent upon the initial conditions they experience as they bundle together as a quanta. That is a mouthful of words that can be summed up in the word "sponge." As the energy particles bundle together, they absorb the conditions around them and that determines the form the quanta takes.

Let me illustrate this with a simple quanta—a snowflake. Its initial conditions are the wind speed, moisture content, and temperature at the points in the cloud where it starts to form and continues to do so as it falls. The unique combination of conditions at those points is what makes the snowflake into its unique shape.

Your Human Sponge Time

The time when people absorb initial conditions is from the time the brain starts to develop, shortly after conception, until the age of two and a half. The initial conditions you were absorbing were how the people around you felt about being themselves—not what they said or did. Of course, the times when people feel intense emotions often coincide with intense behavior, but the feeling was what your brain took in.

You absorbed how they felt about being human and that determined how you feel about being yourself to this very day.

What Should Have Happened During Your Sponge Time

The kernel of energy at your core, what you started out with, is what Quanta Change calls "natural well-being." It's the feeling that you are *great* just being yourself. What should have happened from conception until age two and a half was that you absorbed how *great* everyone around you felt about being themselves. As you soaked it up, that wonderful feeling would allow your core well-being to expand and harmonize with the people around you. It would allow you to become a unique expression of natural well-being that fit in well with all those great-feeling people.

What's that? Did I just hear you say, "Uh-oh!"? *Sigh*. Yeah. You might be thinking, "My parents had some pretty rough days when I was little." Or you might even be thinking, "The people taking care of me had nothing *but* rough days! Oh, no! I absorbed all of that?" Even if you came from a family of folks who felt pretty good about life, everyone has some tough days here and there, and you were absorbing that alongside all the other good stuff.

But what if you experienced abuse or neglect when you were young? Someone who abuses anyone, especially a child, is acting out of an extreme level of Learned Distress. And the negative feelings a child absorbs are equally as intense. If this was your experience, I'm so incredibly sorry. And you are not alone. I experienced childhood abuse and neglect, as did many of my clients. And fortunately, I have found from my own and my clients' cases that Quanta Change can help you unlearn the Learned Distress that you absorbed from those intense situations. Or, as one client described it, Quanta Change allowed her to move from "the monster always waiting for me after brief glimpses of relief or joy," to saying, "freedom from the chains of pain and fear handed down family lines is possible."

Sponges Can't Choose

If you plop a sponge into a mixed dish of water and soda pop, the sponge is going to absorb it all, right? The sponge can't say, "I'll take the water, thanks! But that soda has way too much sugar, so that would be a bad choice."

The same is true of your baby sponge-brain. The rational brain doesn't even start to develop until age two and a half, so while you're in sponge mode you have no choice about the feelings you absorb from others. You don't have the ability to say, "Mom was sick, and Dad got the groceries and tripped over the dog when he got home, and the milk spilled everywhere, which the dog tracked onto the clean carpet, and now everyone is upset and having a really bad day. That seems like a lot of icky feelings to absorb. I'd better just leave it alone."

Nope. You absorbed it all, and as it came in it became personal to you—it became the feeling that "there is something wrong with *me*." This awful feeling is Learned Distress.

As you absorbed Learned Distress, your brain developed your way of fitting well, like an interlocking puzzle piece, with that awful feeling and with those people who were feeling bad around you. This is your survival mechanism, and it's an important part of what Quanta Change addresses.

Quanta Change Is a No-Blame Zone

I have two pieces of good news.

One: I'm sure you can agree now that you didn't choose to absorb Learned Distress, right? In your sponge-like time, you didn't have a choice and so it isn't your fault that you feel bad—that you feel in some way, shape, or form like something is wrong with you. Take a moment to sit with that. It is *not your fault* that you feel bad about being yourself. There is nothing you could have done to avoid that. Whew!

Two: It's not your parents' or other early caregivers' fault, either. They absorbed Learned Distress before they had any choice from their parents, as their parents did from theirs, and back into eternity. And sometimes people act in very intense ways while feeling their Learned Distress. That does *not* make abusive behavior acceptable in any way, and it might be important or necessary to hold them accountable for their behavior. And yet I can say from deeply painful personal experience that it can *also* be helpful to recognize that they were acting in ways that were beyond their rational control.

I realize that you might be feeling a bit of disappointment. It can feel good—even cathartic—to know who you can blame for feeling bad, right? When we feel lousy, railing against the person we think is to blame can feel really helpful in the moment.

I'm all for catharsis, but my experience is that it is possible to move way beyond that blame, which never fixes anything or does more than help us temporarily blow out a little anger and frustration. No matter who we absorbed it from, Learned Distress is stored inside us now. That might feel scary to you, but it gives you the amazing opportunity to actually get rid of it. That's the great news!

Your Sense of Self

You've arrived! You're now two and a half years old and you have a formed sense of self that stores how you feel about being yourself. It's like a bucket that contains two kinds of feeling: natural well-being, or the feeling that you are just great being yourself, and Learned Distress, the feeling that there's something wrong with you being just the way you are. Your survival mechanism is contained within the Learned Distress side of the bucket. This sense-of-self bucket containing well-being and Learned Distress is what your brain draws on to automatically generate the moments of your life.

Is that making sense? The answer to the question of why you feel bad about being yourself is that early in life you absorbed the feeling that something is wrong with you and it got trapped in your sense of self. It's not your fault and it's no one else's fault. But you're going to learn how you can ladle Learned Distress out of that sense-of-self bucket so you can feel better. First, though, you will come to understand how that stored negative feeling has kept making you feel bad and has made negative patterns happen in your life. That's coming in the next chapter!

What It's Costing You to Not Solve This Problem

Maybe you're thinking that once you get a better handle on your Learned Distress and survival mechanism, you can just work a little harder to make things better. What I will help you understand in these next chapters is that your pattern and its negative consequences just keep intensifying over time unless you unlearn their source.

This building intensity could mean a number of things in your day-to-day life. You might just keep feeling worse—more frustrated, exhausted, anxious, depressed, or angry that your hard work to feel better isn't paying off. You might see some part of your life fall apart in a way that you can't put back together, like a relationship, a job, or your health. Or if everything I've just said has been your experience for a while, your life might continue to get more difficult. Sorry! I take no joy in telling you this. But I have so much good news to share, so keep reading!

My Vision for You

If you have tried many methods of feeling better and making your life work better but still not found the results you seek, what I want you to know is that you really can tap into the well-being at your core more easily than you have been able to before. I want you to experience the joy and ease that my clients describe to me every day as they unlearn layers of the feeling that there's something wrong with them. Here's what that can look like.

You wake up with an underlying sense of peace you never have experienced before. You have faith that you are *already* good enough just being yourself. You trust yourself in a way you never have before. You feel more comfortable sharing who you really are with people, and the more you are able to automatically show up being yourself, the more others find they can be themselves. This is unconditional love in action.

Why Is It So Hard to Feel Good Just Being You?

You realize that the thing you've always believed you *had* to do—like taking care of everyone else while ignoring your own needs, or cleaning up the kitchen counter the moment you're done eating, or worrying about something you *always* worry about—you wake up one day and think, "Oh! I don't have to do that!" It's nothing you planned or laid out or talked to your coach about. It has just somehow been removed from your plate. And you don't even feel guilty about it!

Your happiness is decoupled from making or having things be a certain way. You feel that you can be happy *now*, no matter how many items remain on your to-do list, whether that's cleaning the kitchen or writing your novel or finding your life partner. That elusive "live in the now" that you've always heard about but haven't quite been able to touch? You actually have that experience more and more often. And the funny thing is that the better you feel about being yourself *now*, the more those things that really matter to you can fall into place.

In ways you did nothing to bring about, people may start treating you better, start listening to you more, start asking what's important to you and including you more, and show you that you are of value in a way you've never experienced. You may find that you can speak up for yourself in ways you never have and you are met with respect. This might be shocking if you've experienced great pushback when standing up for yourself.

It gets easier to accomplish things, large and small. In fact, some things might happen so easily that you don't even realize it until a friend says, "What do you mean you cleaned out the garage this weekend? You've been complaining about not being able to do that for 15 years! Who are you and what have you done with my friend?!"

Some part of your life that was stuck or blocked or tangled starts to work better. You're amazed because you've been trying to fix that for years, maybe decades! You wish you could have done it sooner, but you're so glad that finally this part of your life feels and works better.

What really has meaning for you becomes much more obvious, and this clears up longstanding questions about your career or relationships. You feel that you can act on what matters to you, maybe for the first time. You have a new sense of power to take your life in the direction that really fulfills you, and as so often is the case, that also benefits the people around you, your community, and the world in ways you hadn't imagined were possible.

But, What If ...?

Are you feeling apprehensive? Wondering if the vision I've just laid out for you really is possible? Are you feeling some familiar fear that often comes up when you're considering something new?

Well, none of that is surprising. Your survival mechanism holds on for dear life. So it wants to keep you headed in the same direction you have been, and you're probably hearing the familiar voice say, "Nothing ever works for you, so why would this be any different?" or, "This might be too overwhelming," or, "Things aren't really that bad, so I'll just work a little harder on my gratitude journal."

No matter what that voice is saying, what I can tell you is that I have helped many people, even the "nothing ever works for me" person, experience the changes I described above. They've found themselves profoundly relieved to feel different and better at last. Finally, things worked more easily than they'd ever experienced. If you're frustrated and exhausted by working desperately hard to feel better without any payoff, you can experience those changes, too.

Quick Summary of What's to Come

In the upcoming chapters, I'll share a bit of who I am and my own Quanta Change journey, so you'll know that I am always walking alongside you, always helping you understand the shift to well-being from having been through this transition myself. Then, we're going to dive deeply into this work, first to deepen your understanding of how you got where you are and how Quanta Change can help you feel better, and then to show you the "box" that your negative stuff fits into, your Quanta Change Sensory Quotient. Lest you fear this is just another exercise in understanding the misery, I can assure you that the entire focus of this book is on getting you out of that miserable "box" so you can truly experience your well-being!

I'll also address the ways your shift to well-being could be a little bumpy at times, with support for smoothing over those bumps. And I'll share how you can take the next big step toward feeling better and having your life work more easily. Let's go!

CHAPTER 2

Why Do Negative Situations and Patterns Keep Happening Despite Your Best Efforts to Stop Them?

Is there some negative feeling that keeps cropping up inside you or some negative situation you just can't seem to stop from repeating? Perhaps no matter how many to-do lists you make, you just can't get your house organized. Or no matter how carefully you screen the people you date, you keep ending up in the same abusive relationship.

You're very clear that you don't want to keep experiencing this and you've tried to stop it. Over and over. But it just keeps rolling and you can't figure out why.

In this chapter, I'll use the discoveries from Phase Two of the Quanta Change research to solve that mystery for you. Sir Isaac Newton is going to help me. Specifically, we're going to look at how his Third Law of Motion explains how all of the situations and patterns in your life are generated automatically out of your sense of self.

Equal and Opposite Misery

Newton's Third Law states that "for every action, there's an equal and opposite reaction." If you've heard this law related to how our lives work before, I ask you to put on your "beginner's mind" right now. I want to make sure that you really understand the Quanta Change take on this law fully.

In this case, the *action* was you absorbing Learned Distress—that negative feeling came *in*. Then, that feeling heads back *out* (*opposite* reaction) as your brain uses the feeling or energy stored in your sense of self to generate moments that feel the *same* (or *equal*) to the feeling you stored early in life. There's the equal and opposite reaction.

Let's say that you absorbed the feeling early in life that there's never enough for you. Your brain will continue to generate moments in which you feel the same way, whether it's never enough time, enough money, enough energy, enough food, or something else.

Here's an example from my childhood. My dad was very sick and so my mom's attention just had to be more focused on him sometimes. I can trace back to that a continual feeling that "I never get enough attention from others." I even got two degrees in violin performance and made that my first career to try and overcome that feeling—I mean, if you're on stage performing people *have* to give you their attention, right? And yet after years and years of performing, I still felt that utter lack of people seeing me and hearing me!

Permanently Set to Repeat

There's a word that I wish I could go back and ask Sir Isaac to add to his law: "automatic." So Newton's Third Law would read, "For every action, there is an equal, opposite, and automatic reaction." It's implied, but our human tendency to want to get in there and control things can make us feel like we could have some say over the equal and opposite reaction. If we just *try* hard enough, we could interrupt it or divert it in a better direction.

And you may have had some success with at least putting some controls around the equal and opposite reaction output—if your survival mechanism allows for control mechanisms to work. There are lots of ways to temporarily hem in the Learned Distress equal and opposite reaction. Maybe you've experienced that. You find a new practice or routine and for a while, you feel better. You think, "Finally, I've found my way and I can finally relax and be happy!" Or you might instead think, "At least I have that icky feeling managed now!"

And then, it takes more and more of that same work to keep things going in the right direction. Or maybe it stops working altogether. And you're back in the same frustrating place. Right?

How Learned Distress Has Won (Until Now)

I'll never forget the way that Quanta Change founder Mimi Herrmann described this phenomenon. She said that Learned Distress is patiently indifferent to all of the blocks you put in its way. It's like water running downhill. You can put a log in front of it. You can build a wall in front of it. You can put the Hoover Dam in front of it. That water is still going to make it all the way down the hill.

Learned Distress is the same. It eventually makes its way *out* (getting back to the equal and opposite reaction), and as it does, you feel it in some way—maybe you feel anxious, depressed, or angry, or something is going wrong in your relationships, career, or health, or how you express yourself, or how you live your life.

The Bumpy Learned Distress Road

Here's one more way to picture how the equal and opposite reaction works. It might sound a little scary at first, but I promise not to leave you in the scary place for long! Okay, ready? There is a two-year-old in the proverbial driver's seat of your life. I know, yikes! It's the one inside of you—your sense of self, the part of you that stores how you feel about being yourself. The equal and opposite reaction allows the two-year-old to drive on one of two roads—the well-being road, a pleasant, scenic excursion; or the Learned Distress road, a bumpy ride at the *very* best.

Your survival mechanism may have allowed you to exert some temporary control over the toddler's driving. Or you might now be thinking about how various methods seemed to keep you on the well-being road for a long time. You might be thinking, "Why did meditation or affirmations or (fill in the blank) work for a long time but then they stopped working? Because, Sara, I am now getting very familiar with the potholed side street and I just want to go back to the way it used to be!"

The bad news is that Quanta Change can't take the two-year-old sense of self out of the driver's seat. Sorry! But the good news is that it can give you more say than you've ever had before about which road the two-year-old takes you down from day to day. In fact, the Quanta Change process will *move* the two-year-old over to the well-being road for you. This means that more often you'll wake up for an enjoyable, scenic drive instead of a harrowing misadventure on a perilous side street.

And this process is *not* about learning to cajole a toddler into doing what you want them to do. It's not about trying to control them, convince them, reform them, bribe them, or outright demand better behavior. Thank goodness! It is about making a deep change in you that automatically puts that toddler on the well-being road more and more of the time, and that allows you to feel much better than controlling their driving ever did.

It's Not Your Fault!

Has anyone ever asked you why you're choosing to be sick or depressed or be in an abusive relationship or (fill in the blank)? This drives me nuts! Well, honestly, it makes me angry. No one would ever choose to feel awful or continually put themselves back in the same terrible situation. No one. It breaks my heart when someone tells me that they not only feel lousy but then on top of it, they feel they should have been able to change or stop it.

If you've been beating yourself up about something you haven't been able to change, consider this: Even if you could have tried harder (and I'm pretty sure you have tried as hard as you could), the Learned Distress would still be winning. The equal and opposite reaction, functioning automatically, keeps generating your life experiences by drawing from the Learned Distress bucket inside you. When that happens, you can feel awful in ways that are beyond your rational input or control.

My good news is that there is a well-being bucket in your sense of self, too, and there is a way for the equal and opposite reaction to start pulling from it instead. I want to share some of my own Quanta Change story now to help you see what that shift looks like.

Sara's Bumpy Road

By my late 20s, I had felt the urgent need for change in several areas of my life for years, even decades. Really, it felt like *everything* about me needed to change, but I could write a whole book just on that, so I'll boil it down to four big things.

First, my dependence on other people's approval was overwhelming. Everything I did and said was geared toward achieving that goal. As I have found is true for many of my clients, my very survival felt like it relied on doing everything perfectly in a way that would make other people happy. While it can be a common experience that fades after high school, that pressure only intensified the older I got.

I used to lose sleep—sometimes multiple nights of sleep—over what someone thought of some little thing I had said or done. I would re-explain myself over and over in letters, emails, and voicemails. I'm cringing just thinking about it! Of course, this often just drove people away, and even though I knew that, I couldn't stop myself.

I pursued my first career mostly because playing the violin was a way that I could win approval—from my parents, teachers, orchestra conductors, and friends, and random people I met who thought it was really cool. There are wonderful things about playing music for a living, but it became more apparent as I moved further into my career that there was a problem. I no longer had weekly approval-seeking violin lessons, and the more I worked with symphony conductors who didn't garner my respect much less the desire for their approval, the more I realized that there was an emptiness to all the practicing it takes to play at a high level. It was hard to admit to myself that I had spent hours a day in a practice room, every day for a couple of decades, just to get people to like me. But it was true.

And, getting approval wasn't the end goal—survival was. There were people-shaped holes in my life caused by the feeling that I didn't matter and that I couldn't accomplish things on my own. So doing things perfectly to gain their approval was all for the purpose of them filling those holes in some way or helping me in ways I couldn't help myself. As you might imagine, that strategy never really worked, and I felt increasingly alone and without the means to achieve my goals.

The second big issue that had vexed me for years was poor sleep. I remember having trouble sleeping as early as elementary school. Through college and beyond, my sleep pattern deteriorated to sleeping for a few hours, waking up in the middle of the night and worrying—usually about what someone else thought of me!—and, if I was lucky, going back to sleep for another couple of hours before the alarm went off. I came to dread bedtime. (If you can relate, there's hope! You'll read more in the coming chapters.)

The third big issue was adrenal fatigue and overall endocrine suppression. I could remember symptoms of it going back to age seven or eight. I had a whole constellation of symptoms—I was always cold, I often nearly blacked out upon standing, my hair was falling out, I couldn't lose weight, and many more. I realized I'd gotten a lot worse one summer when I was a fellow at the Aspen Music Festival. I could no longer think quickly enough to keep up with the conductor's beat, and I couldn't keep up in string quartet music that I had played dozens of times for weddings. That brain fog scared me way more than all of the symptoms I'd had for a couple of decades.

Losing even a fraction of a second here and there will end a violin career.

The fourth issue was my career itself. Beyond my difficulties playing because of my illness, I was burning out. But what else was I going to do? Two decades of practicing, two college degrees, countless lessons and summer festivals (summer school for musicians), and I had no idea how else I could make a living, much less what I *wanted* to do. What was my real purpose on the planet? I didn't have a clue.

The Try-to-Fix-It Years

Although it wasn't the decades of work many of my clients have done, I did spend my late 20s doing various kinds of self-help and therapy work to try and stop the people-pleasing. But it kept intensifying—more worry, more sleepless nights, more obsessive emails, trying to find new ways to get people to like me. I knew that I shouldn't *need* people's approval, that I should be able to support myself emotionally and behave as an equal in my various relationships. But no matter how many ways I learned to try and do those things, I still felt "less than," dependent and needy, and I acted accordingly. It felt like I was banging my head against a wall and I was hopeless. As you might guess, that didn't help me sleep any better at night.

As for the hormone issues, I had tried nearly all of the traditional and alternative medical approaches to it, including the supplement regimen of one of the foremost experts on adrenal fatigue. It included taking about 80 pills a day, which I dutifully choked down for months. When I flew across the country for a follow-up appointment, this doctor ran his assessments and said, "You should taper off my regimen. It's not working for you. I don't know what else to tell you to try."

My only option left was "blocking and replacing" all of my hormones—essentially going on hormonal life support at the age of 29. By that time, I had noticed that when I blocked and replaced one hormone, some other hormone would tank and I would feel even worse than before. It dawned on me that some force working at a more fundamental level was dragging me on this downward physical trajectory, no matter what block I tried to put in its way. I wondered what that force might do if I shut off its endocrine pathway, and I didn't really want to find out!

And, as for finding my purpose in life beyond playing the violin, I was lost. It seemed that any other career would be just like music—that it would take 20 years to master. And I really had no idea what I wanted to do instead. I'd learned a lot in trying to solve my hormone issues so I sometimes sounded like a doctor talking about it, and friends suggested medical school. Others noted that I was a good listener—maybe I should become a therapist? I was so tired and brain-fogged from the adrenal fatigue that I sobbed at the thought of the energy either of those training paths would take. I stayed lost a while longer.

The Conversation That Changed Everything

Those problems were pretty scattered across the areas of my life, so I was shocked when I met Mimi Herrmann and learned that they all stemmed from the same place. How was it possible that people pleasing, sleep problems, adrenal fatigue, and a lack of direction in life could have a common root? I listened with skepticism. But she was pretty convincing. She explained Learned Distress to me and a light bulb went off. Feeling like there was something wrong with me? That sounded familiar!

Even more surprising than identifying the root problem, she told me there was a way to get rid of Learned Distress permanently. Once she had described her research and change process, I felt a glimmer of hope. I'd been trying so hard to feel better in so many ways for so long that I was a little—okay, maybe a lot—afraid to believe it. I bet you might be familiar with that particular fear yourself! But I remember thinking that day, "If what she's saying about Quanta Change is true, she has the way through that wall I've been beating my head against for years. Wow!"

I summoned my courage and started into my own Quanta Change process with Mimi as my guide. We started to identify the Learned Distress at the heart of my frustrations and roadblocks, starting with my Sensory Quotient pattern, the Caregiver, which you'll learn much more about later when we explore the five other SQ patterns. Turns out, people with this Learned Distress pattern don't feel capable within themselves so they work hard to please others in hopes of getting the companionship and assistance they *need*. Mimi said her alternate name for Caregiver pattern was "Manipulator." Ouch! I mean, well, yeah . . . but did she have to say it out loud? But she showed me how there is no blame or malicious intent behind Learned Distress. It's just the only way we have of surviving.

She said that Learned Distress, in general, is incompatible with getting adequate, effective sleep. It's a fear ("something is wrong with me") trapped inside of us that keeps us on high alert. Caregivers tend to be very aware of their Learned Distress—even feel immersed or drowning in it—and having Learned Distress up at the surface like that was keeping my brain at attention, ready to try and fix what was wrong with me. She'd checked box number two in the problems list!

Caregivers are often sick or have something wrong physically in their survival mechanism's attempt to get assistance from others. She explained that this was nothing I could have chosen or made happen, which was a relief. We even identified specific early childhood sources of my illness. The first was my father's illness and death when I was young. We absorb "how it is to be human" from the people around us early in life, and then our lives unfold on that blueprint in some way. My diabetic dad was diagnosed with kidney failure the same week my mom found out she was pregnant with me, and he died when I was three and a half. So what I absorbed was that the "way to be an adult" is to get sick and die. And I did such a good job carrying out the blueprint! By age 29, I was headed for hormonal life support, despite my very best efforts to the contrary.

A second childhood source of my endocrine issues was from my mom. She was a brilliant, talented woman. And she really struggled in some ways. One of the ways she experienced her own Learned Distress was intense anxiety, diagnosed much later in her life. It wasn't safe to be "too anything" around her—too loud, too sad, too angry, too needy, too happy. (Everything a baby is!) Anything could set her off, and she expressed her anxiety in angry ways that took me a long time to understand and admit was verbal and emotional abuse. A baby's sense of self develops to survive well with her people. The way I survived well with my anxious mom was to stay really quiet and small. Of course, there was no way for my baby brain to say, "I'll keep myself under wraps now and then once I turn 18 and get out of here I'll open right back up!" When I learned from the work of Dr. Elizabeth Vliet that what a fully functional endocrine system does is allow one to be a fully expressive human being, I finally understood what happened when I was so young. My baby brain shut down my hormones to keep me quiet and small.

There was one more facet from the combination of my parents' issues that led to my illness. My anxious mom, whose Learned Distress made parenting a baby such a challenge, was taking care of a very sick man and working full-time as a newspaper editor. I have no doubt that she gave me every possible moment of attention she could. And yet I also know there were times when she left me with a neighbor in a hurry (or panic) so she could rush my dad to the hospital. He needed an increasing amount of care, and what I absorbed from all of this was "the sick person gets the love." Is it any wonder that by my late 20s I sobbingly blurted out to a man I was interested in dating, "I just want someone to take care of me!"?

But what about my lack of knowing what to do with my life? Turns out that Caregivers are entirely focused on everyone else in order to survive. Their Learned Distress pattern actually buries the ability to really know who they are, what matters to them, and what they really want to do and say. Well, there it was. Mimi actually had covered all four wildly divergent problems under the umbrella of Learned Distress.

The Change I've Experienced

First, as most people do who have struggled with sleep when starting Quanta Change, I started to sleep better right away. And the shift from fragmented sleep (my pattern for so many years) to sleeping through the night pretty consistently happened within a few months.

My shift in needing people's approval had some points that are pretty typical in this process. Namely, they were *weird*. I can remember right where I was standing when it hit me that I didn't actually care what a particular person thought of me—a guy whose approval and love I had desperately wanted. When a big layer of Learned Distress is peeled off, it can really be discombobulating, even to the point of feeling like you couldn't get that dysfunction back if you really tried. And it's been years since I lost sleep over what someone thinks of me.

It's so much bigger than the absence of approval-seeking, though. I used to feel like *everything* was wrong with me. Starting in grade school, I cried myself to sleep almost every night. Today, I love who I am. I am strong and confident in who I am and what I have to offer the world. And it's based on what I know and think, not on what someone else is telling me to think. I look to others now for collaboration based on the gifts they can bring. I love my life. It feels whole and complete and full. There are no people-shaped holes anymore. I'm not searching for *the* life partner who is going to fix everything. I'm open to the idea of a new relationship at some point, but if that man shows up our relationship will have to fit really well within this life I already love, and it will be about sharing my already-great life in ways that are good for both of us.

And I have one more triumph to share in this needing-approval arena. I've been overweight since infancy. For much of my life, I believed what the so-called experts said (which research is now debunking)—that if I ate less, ate more, ate differently, exercised this way, or that way, or all the ways, or doubled it, I could reach some "goal weight" and stay there. I cried into my pillow over this more than anything else. My day was a triumph or tragedy based on a half-pound difference on the scale—for *years*. My body shape was the number one reason I *knew* that I could never be perfect enough to get everyone's approval. My Quanta Change on this is something I couldn't have dreamed of. I actually feel good enough being myself *in this body*. Instead of constant self-loathing and attempts at shrinking my poor, long-hated body, my focus is on taking really good care of myself and on *feeling* good.

As for the adrenal fatigue, I started to feel better within weeks. Within a few months, the symptoms I had going all the way back to elementary school had either disappeared entirely or were so reduced that I hardly noticed them. They have never returned.

And finally, the career direction issue. I found that I *loved* diving into where my own Learned Distress patterns came from. Friends had urged me toward medical or psychology school. But here, right in front of me was a process that was helping me solve both my biggest emotional and physical struggles, one that was based in research on addressing why people get sick and feel bad in the first place. I was a little nervous the day I told Mimi that I wanted to help people the way she was helping me—that I had found my life's purpose and it was being a Quanta Change Guide. What if she said no to my life's purpose? That would be the ultimate in disapproval! To my great relief and joy, she welcomed the idea, and I spent almost five more years learning from her, working with her to further refine the process and starting to help others uncover their natural well-being. Nothing I've ever done has felt so joyous and natural to me as guiding others through this process. And what's so ironic is that doing this work feels to me like what non-musicians imagine playing the violin for a living is like—it's creative, fun, and energizing.

Why I Want to Help You

The best way I can convey how Quanta Change *feels* is that it's like turning down the volume on a radio. You know the things that have been turned up to 11 in your life? Imagine twisting the knob way down, so instead of screaming in your ear, they're a whisper at best.

I'll share one more of my own changes that I always think of when I talk about turning down the volume. This Learned Distress was triggered by the end of any kind of relationship with a man, including situations like my violin teacher moving to a different university, in addition to the obvious romantic disappointments or endings. It goes right back to my dad dying when I was three and a half. It's easy to see why, right?

At its height, on a scale of one to ten, this one had gotten to the point of screeching at a 14 for months at a time. While I wasn't at the point of planning it or acting on it, I thought a lot about what a relief it would be to have my life end. I welcomed a tree to fall on me and put me out of my misery.

Since I started Quanta Change, I've had several big layers of this Learned Distress peel off as some relationship or another ended. I'll fast-forward to the last one. If you'd compared it on paper to my other breakups, you would have guessed that I was at least back up to 14 on the misery dial. And I did have some rough days for a few months. But the hardest days might have, at most, hit a seven or eight and lasted for a couple of hours. And not once did I ever feel that old, familiar, persistent devastation of "I should just be gone.

The only solution to this pain is to stop existing." Not for a single second.

I get the joy every day of helping other people turn down their own dial. I get to hear people say, "I've worked on myself for decades and I've never felt this good ever before." "I feel an underlying sense of peace I've never experienced." "I love myself, and I deserve to have a good life—I've never felt that way before!" "My husband and I are really talking and getting to know each other for the first time." "I know for the first time that I matter, and people are actually treating me better!"

Now, let's continue to move through how you got to where you are right now and how you can experience these same kinds of shifts in your life!

CHAPTER 3

How Is Sleep Perpetuating Your Negative Patterns?

I know, I know... "Sleep is perpetuating my problems? I thought sleep was good for me! Sara, how much longer until the good news you keep writing about finally gets here?!" Just hang in with me a bit longer. It's coming very soon. First, it's key that you understand how Learned Distress has hung on for so long in your sense of self.

Phase Three of the Quanta Change research identified sleep and wakefulness as two distinct energy states, and it identified the very important work that takes place during sleep, which I'll lay out for you in this chapter.

The equal and opposite reaction creates a need in your sense of self. It means that the feeling or energy stored there gets depleted every day as it is used to generate your life. You might think, "Well, great, Sara! Learned Distress depleted = problem solved! Right?" Unfortunately, no. You need that energy in your sense of self to live out every day of your life. And just as you recharge your phone battery when it is depleted, you recharge your sense of self every day.

The Human Recharging Station

You plug your phone into an outlet to charge it. Sleep is what you plug yourself into in order to recharge on several levels.

Physical recharging happens during deep sleep, the slowest level of brain wave activity. This is when you get the most human growth hormone release during the day, which helps rejuvenate and repair your body. Mental recharging happens during the middle level of brain wave activity.

The fastest level of brain wave activity is what Quanta Change is most focused on. It is Rapid Eye Movement sleep or REM sleep, which is when you dream. A crucial Quanta Change research discovery was that this is the time when your sense of self—how you feel about being yourself—gets recharged.

Human Recharging Fuel

You recharge your phone with electricity. The energy that recharges your sense of self each night is derived from the most intense feelings you experienced that day. I'd like you to imagine a day in which three great things happened and one awful thing happened. Without looking at your vision board, pulling out your gratitude journal, calling your best friend for a pep talk, or saying your prayers, what are you most focused on? The good stuff or the bad stuff?

It's the bad stuff, right? (And to be clear, the bad stuff includes how you're planning to deal with the thing that went wrong today.) This is the concept widely known as negativity bias. If you remember that Learned Distress exists to protect your survival, focusing intensely on what felt or went wrong today makes sense.

How Is Sleep Perpetuating Your Negative Patterns?

If you were a hunter-gatherer and you just barely outran the water buffalo today, it would be ridiculous to pull out your Stone Age gratitude journal! This is a time for action to make sure you don't have that close a call again. Maybe you need to take a different route tomorrow, or maybe it's time to hang up the spear and let Junior take over. In any case, your survival depends on fixing what went wrong today.

The sense of self is always two and a half years old, which means it has no rational, thinking capacity. It has no way of understanding that writing an imperfect work email is any less a threat to your survival than the water buffalo. So, the sense of self says, "Pay attention! Don't lose sight of this threat!" And you go to sleep plugged into that awful feeling and you recharge your sense of self with it.

Pop quiz (open book style)! Where did the negative feeling or situation come from that day?

Answer: From the equal and opposite reaction pulling out of the danged Learned Distress bucket, right? The Learned Distress is going through a continual revolving door, getting recharged every night.

This actually describes part of the Law of Conservation of Energy, which states that "Energy is neither created nor destroyed, but only transformed into renewable or nonrenewable energy." Usually, renewable energy is the good kind, but not in this case. Renewing Learned Distress every night has perpetuated the various kinds of misery it causes.

Rising Intensity

I have just one more bit of bad news, but I bet it will solve another mystery for you. This comes from an observation that Herrmann made throughout her research, which was that research subjects displayed a rising level of intensity in the manifestations of their Learned Distress. That is because as Learned Distress renews while you sleep, it doesn't just fill the bucket back up to the old line; it actually fills up a little more every night.

This takes us back to the equal and opposite reaction for a moment. Before, I said that the situations that are generated from Learned Distress are an equal reaction in that they feel the same way, or they have the same quality to them, like always feeling like there's never enough. What's also true is that automatically generated feelings and situations are equal to the *intensity* of the stored Learned Distress. So, as that stored intensity rises slightly each night, the intensity of the feelings or situations is also more intense.

To go back to my own example, one way I noticed the rising intensity of "never enough attention from others" was that I experienced more and more pushback and rejection from people whose attention I sought and worked hard to get. I was doing everything I knew to win their approval, and I felt like I mattered less and less to them.

Have You Felt This Rising Level of Learned Distress?

Have you continued to do all the right things but feel like it's getting harder to get the desired outcome? You're hanging in there, but you're starting to get a little (or a lot) tired!

How Is Sleep Perpetuating Your Negative Patterns?

Or does it seem that getting the right outcome is still possible but you just feel worse?

Or maybe you're thinking back to a breaking-point moment: Before, you felt good and things worked well, but after, things seemed to fall apart in some or even many ways.

Or you might be saying that things just feel worse and things work less well over time no matter what you do. You might even get to the point of wondering if there's even a purpose in trying to feel better or overcome negative situations.

You've waited a long time, and I'm happy to say that the good news of Quanta Change starts in the next chapter!

CHAPTER 4

Why Hasn't Everything You've Tried to Feel Better Worked?

The first piece of good news I have for you is that it is *not your fault* that the practices, techniques, methods, and therapies you've worked so hard at and hoped would solve your problems haven't worked. I know how frustrating it is to try so hard to feel better and not see results for a long time, if at all. And then, on top of that disappointment, if you're like me and lots of my clients, you beat yourself up for not having done it right or perfectly enough or often enough, and you feel even worse!

I hope you'll let yourself off the hook. It's not your fault!

Fireside Chat

The second piece of good news I have comes straight from the Law of Conservation of Energy. (If there's a physicist nearby, feel free to give them a hug because this is great news!) You might remember that the law says, "Energy is neither created nor destroyed, but only transformed into renewable or nonrenewable energy." In the last chapter, you learned how Learned Distress is turned into renewable energy every night when you go to sleep and your sense of self is recharged with the bad feelings you've experienced during the day.

Now it's time to look at the nonrenewable part of that law. A great example of nonrenewable energy is burning a log in a fireplace. Once you've burned the log, you have ashes that can no longer generate heat.

During the Quanta Change research, this tiny piece of one law created a lot of excitement! What if you could burn Learned Distress off like a log in a fireplace so that the Learned Distress "ashes" could no longer be used to generate negative feelings and situations? What if the equal and opposite reaction no longer had so much Learned Distress to draw upon? What if that meant that your two-year-old sense of self could switch over to driving on the well-being road? That would be amazing!

A Significant Roadblock

The research had identified a big problem, though. When your rational, thinking brain is operating there is a wall of resistance that blocks deep change from happening.

I bet you're familiar with this roadblock. Think about some frustrating feeling you've dealt with. It might be feeling like you need to be perfect, that it's *so hard* to accomplish things, that you always have to be the best at things, or something else. You know what it is for you. Have you ever been able to think your way out of it? If so, for how long? Did that stick for more than a day or a few days? Or did you have to keep hammering away at that negative feeling, only keeping it at bay for a short time until it took over again?

That inability to think your way out of Learned Distress is evidence of the roadblock in action. Have you maybe even found that the roadblock has a voice and that it likes to talk back to you? "Oh, you just want things to work easily? Really? Have you noticed how it's *always* been hard to get things done? You think that's going to change now? Um, no, we're just going to keep doing it that way, okay?" The roadblock can be very mouthy!

The Reason for the Wall of Resistance

The roadblock, that wall of resistance to change, is actually there for a good reason. It protects your survival mechanism. Remember how that survival mechanism got put into place before the age of two and a half, before you had any rational processing capacity? When you look at the survival mechanism now through your rational brain lens, some of it might seem pretty cockamamie. Like the part of my survival mechanism, absorbed straight from my father being very ill and dying when I was little, that said, "The way to live well and survive as an adult human is to get sick and die."

It sounds crazy, right? But, my two-year-old brain had no way of knowing that, and the wall of resistance to change was there to protect my survival mechanism at all costs. Before I unlearned that big chunk of Learned Distress, my two-year-old sense of self was blithely driving me down the Learned Distress road, "helping me to survive" the only way it knew how to, and I was getting sicker and sicker, despite all of my efforts to get better.

It's why this weird thing happened when one of the best endocrine doctors in the country said, "Sara, my regimen of supplements to heal the adrenals usually works, but it's not working for you." Part of me was discouraged and depressed. But there was also a pretty strong voice inside that was leaping for joy, exclaiming, "Great job, Sara! You're right on track!" Um, what?!

Here's another example you've probably heard. A baby is being abused and the authorities have arrived to take her to a place we all know will be instantly better for her. But she's clinging for dear life to the person who has been abusing her. Why? Because that is the only survival she's ever known. The two-year-old sense of self who is in the driver's seat of your life is no different, and it will cling as tightly as possible to your survival mechanism to try and keep you safe.

A Curve in the Road to Roadblock Removal

So, again, the Quanta Change research indicated that while your rational brain is operating, you can't get through the wall of resistance to change. So, if the goal was to burn Learned Distress off like a log in a fireplace, the rational brain would need to be out of the way entirely.

Initially, two broad mechanisms were considered, approaches you may have tried: meditation and hypnosis. The hope was that one of these would shut down the roadblock. But, as a hypnotherapist colleague once said to me, during hypnosis or meditation, the rational brain is on a shelf in the corner. It's not entirely shut down, and nearly anything can bring you right back into your rational state, like a truck driving by or your cat jumping up on the bed. Maybe you've experienced just that.

So, back to the drawing board. But the way through the rational brain roadblock—that wall of resistance to change that has been doing its best to keep you alive, all the while being misguided by your Learned Distress—finally became clear. That piece of good news is coming your way next!

I hope that before you turn the page you'll take one more deep breath and remind yourself that what you've just learned shows it is not your fault that you haven't been able to bring about the change you're seeking. And that you're feeling hopeful, knowing that a way to put your two-year-old sense of self on the well-being road is right around the bend.

CHAPTER 5

How Can Sleep Be at the Heart of the Solution to Your Biggest Problems?

We're getting to my favorite part of the science of Quanta Change. I mean, what could be better than delivering the message that this change happens through *sleep*? But, I need to help you understand how you can tap into your sense of self to bring about this change, so don't go to sleep on me just yet!

There are a couple of reasons that sleep is the vehicle to smash through the wall of resistance to change. First, sleep is the time each day that your rational brain is entirely shut down and out of the way. That's when the wall of resistance to change is shut down. This means that we can have free access to your sense of self, that container that stores how you feel about being yourself, both good and bad—both Learned Distress and your natural well-being.

Second, as we just discussed, REM sleep, which is when you dream, is the phase during which your sense of self gets recharged. And it's being recharged with the most intense feeling from the day you just lived. So, maybe you've leaped ahead and you're thinking, "Okay, so I just have to tell my sense of self that I want to recharge with well-being instead of Learned Distress while I sleep. Great! I'll see you later, Sara. I'm headed off to sleep!" Or maybe you've already guessed the next little roadblock encountered in the research and you're hoping I can share a solution.

Between a Rock and a Hard Place

To access the sense of self for deep change, you need the wall of resistance to be shut down, and sleep solves that problem. But you also need to tell your brain that you want to recharge with feeling good instead of feeling bad—with well-being instead of Learned Distress. But you're asleep; how are you supposed to do that?

Amazingly, the ancient Egyptians had their own solution to this problem, and how I wish I could travel back in time and see what kind of results they got. They had sleep temples where priests chanted over the patients to bring about cures for physical and psychological ailments. You'll be relieved to know that Quanta Change does not involve me coming to your house to chant over you while you sleep!

Talking to Your Sense of Self in Its Own Language

In the Quanta Change applied research phase, Herrmann developed a recording to play during sleep to tell your sense of self to recharge with well-being. She also realized that she couldn't just provide an adult, rational message to your sleeping brain about how you want to feel. The sense of self is two and a half years old and it's not one bit rational, right? So, this message would have to come in a way that the two-year-old sense of self could receive it.

Therefore, this Quanta Change Sensory Message recording is a message in the language of dreams, which you can think of as being pictures of feelings. Have you ever awakened after a dream and not been able to make any sense of what it was about? One that had you laughing out loud once you thought about it later because it was total nonsense? That's because the purpose of the dream wasn't to make any rational or narrative sense. It was to take some picture—grabbed from work yesterday, or a history test 40 years ago, or from some movie you watched last weekend—and use it to conjure a feeling so your sense of self could recharge with it.

For instance, I often used to have a dream where I was driving at night on an icy road and it was too dark to see or I couldn't open my eyes to see the road. As you can imagine, I was terrified and felt like I had absolutely no control of where I was going. Once I understood that a part of my survival mechanism was about feeling like I had no ability to achieve what mattered to me—in other words, no ability to control where I was going in life—I could see that this recurring dream recharged that particular piece of Learned Distress each time I had it.

The Quanta Change Sensory Message recording illustrates a particular shift in feeling through different images. In each image, you're feeling bad in some way, and then a shift takes place and you feel better. Something like this: "I'm a leaf floating down a river, and I come to a place where everything is clogged and stagnant, and I'm stuck there. But a current comes and clears the clog out. I float gently into a calm, beautiful pool, surrounded by everything I need and I feel so good here." As you sleep, your brain gets the message that you don't just have to stay with the bad feeling anymore—as your sense of self recharges, you want it to keep shifting more and more to feeling good.

Burning Off Learned Distress for the First Time

During this phase of research, Herrmann had volunteers begin to sleep with the first Sensory Message recording. They filled out reports, which showed a remarkably common set of experiences. In their waking lives, the volunteers were all going through a repeating cycle of change that related to their negative feelings and patterns in some way. Whatever was most intense for them, whether it was in relationships or work or some aspect of daily life, was the area in which the change cycle showed up.

In each change cycle, they felt the Learned Distress as it was being burned off, and then they felt different and better in some way that they didn't work to make happen. They started to say the same kinds of things I've heard my clients say over the past two decades, things like:

"I feel more confident than I ever have at work, and other people are noticing and complimenting me."

"I just know that things are going to be okay."

"I've known for a long time that I didn't need to be perfect, but for the first time, I actually feel good enough just as I am."

"Stuff has been piling up in the garage for years and it was driving me nuts, but I just couldn't get to it. But last Saturday, I walked out there and started picking away at it. Before I knew it, I'd cleaned most of it out. It was so easy that I didn't even recognize myself!"

"I feel more comfortable in my own skin than I ever have, and other people are less overwhelming to me now."

"My whole life has been about making sure everyone else has what they need. But yesterday, I woke up and knew that I was going to come first from now on. And, without neglecting the needs of others who I am responsible for, I'm doing things in a way that meets my needs first. I didn't even think this was possible, and I can't even believe I'm doing it. I feel like a different person."

The research determined that each change cycle burned off a layer of Learned Distress. Participants reported that negative feelings or situations they'd worked on for years actually lessened or changed for the very first time, and that they didn't have to keep working at them day after day. Their change actually "stuck." And, without any effort or direction, natural well-being expanded to take the place of that Learned Distress. Participants reported feeling better and having things work better in ways they didn't try to make happen. Herrmann concluded from these reports that the balance in the sense of self was shifting toward more and more well-being. Incrementally and automatically, the two-year-old switched to driving on the well-being road, instead of the Learned Distress road. Instead of white-knuckling it in the passenger seat or getting out and trying and push the car forward when that ornery two-year-old threw on the parking brake, research participants found they got to relax and enjoy the ride on the road they would most like to be on, their well-being road.

Ensuring the Best Change Cycling Possible

Herrmann and her team were thrilled to see people discover what it was like to live more and more from their well-being. They also noticed a couple of things that needed further attention.

One was the phenomenon that in the day or two after talking through their sleep report with Herrmann, their change cycle intensity ramped up—they had more intense dreams and more intense experiences in various parts of the cycle. It turned out that while the two-year-old sense of self is the one going through the burning off—or unlearning, as it became known—that rational level understanding of Learned Distress and how one wanted to feel instead played an important role in guiding and pushing the sense of self to unlearn.

The second important thing Herrmann noticed was that burning off layers of Learned Distress through this repeating cycle of change could sometimes be intense, overwhelming, or painful. When Learned Distress is headed out, it turns out that you get to feel it. I'll explain more in a bit about how you might experience that—I promise that you'll have plenty of support and that it's worth it!

Eventually, Herrmann and I developed the best way to guide and support you through this process of unlearning Learned Distress and discovering your natural well-being. It consists of the Three Integral Elements of Quanta Change:

Share: Have regular, ongoing phone sessions with a Quanta Change Guide to understand your Learned Distress through your Quanta Change Sensory Quotient pattern(s), understand and receive support through the repeating change cycle, and learn how to tell your brain exactly what you want to change during sleep.

Sleep: Play the Quanta Change Sensory Message recording while you sleep to give your brain your ongoing permission to recharge with well-being instead of Learned Distress. Everyone sleeps with the same recording playing because this is simply the generic catalyst for Quanta Change.

Shift: This simple daytime work is how you tell your brain very specifically what you want to change during sleep. Your Quanta Change Guide will come up with a question that is designed to target the most intense of your Learned Distress as a way of signaling that you want to recharge with the well-being that is its precise opposite. For example, if you said to me that you never have enough time to get everything done, I would suggest this shift question: "What if my well-being always provides enough of everything I need?" Then I would help you understand how to use that question throughout the day to best communicate that message to your sleeping brain.

It is through these Three Integral Elements that my clients tell me every day in some way, "Sara, I feel better than I have ever felt before, and it just happened easily. This is unlike any work on myself that I've ever done before."

You may be getting excited about having that same experience yourself. But, just in case you are actually thinking something more like, "I don't know . . . could that really be true?" the next chapter is just for you. That is *exactly* what I said when I first heard about Quanta Change, and I'm going to answer your question, which is the question I've been answering for myself for the past 20 years.

CHAPTER 6

Change During Sleep—Really? Could It Actually Work for Me?

As you might remember, I was pretty skeptical when my friend told me about Quanta Change while we sat in that Colorado mountain meadow with his wolf-dogs. I remained skeptical after Herrmann walked me through all her research. I've found that everyone doubts at some level that these unprecedented shifts in how you feel and how your life works could really happen at all, not to mention while you *sleep*. For my clients and me, the doubts were eliminated as we experienced change cycle after change cycle that led to feeling so much better. But, if you're having those same questions right now, you're not alone!

The Way It's Been Happening

Question for you: How many times have you started your day with this thought: "If I work really, really hard, today can be a total disaster"? I know it's a weird question so I'll ask it again. How many times have you awakened, thought about how you'd like your day to go, and thought to yourself, "Okay, I'm going to work really hard and hope that I can do *enough* to make myself miserable today! Self, we can do this!"

I can see that look on your face. You're thinking, "Well, the sleep stuff sounded pretty farfetched, but now she just is saying crazy things!" I know this is a weird question to ask you but think about it. You've never put an ounce of effort into making the bad stuff happen—whether it was feeling awful or having something go wrong—right? That stuff happens entirely without any toil on your part, doesn't it? No one desires or chooses to feel bad or have things go wrong in life—*no one*.

The negative feelings, situations, and patterns are effortless because the equal and opposite reaction uses Learned Distress to automatically generate situations for you beyond your rational input or control. In other words, the equal and opposite reaction puts your two-year-old sense of self driving down the Learned Distress road, and you're just along for that miserable, bumpy ride that has gotten worse over time.

Moving to the Well-Being Road— and Why That Can Seem So Fanciful

Each time you go through the Quanta Change cycle, you burn off a layer of Learned Distress, and your natural well-being automatically expands to take its place. That expanded well-being allows for the equal and opposite reaction to draw more often from the well-being bucket to generate situations. This is what puts that two-year-old driver on the well-being road where you feel better and life works more easily.

Change During Sleep—Really? Could It Actually Work for Me?

Even if that makes theoretical sense to you, is it still hard to imagine it actually happening? Here's why: As humans, we're used to putting a lot of work into making ourselves feel good and making good things happen. Think about keeping yourself healthy. If you're like many, you probably started to think about everything you need to do—eat better, exercise more, get to bed earlier—and maybe you're even feeling weary just thinking about all those tasks!

Or, if health comes pretty easily for you, you might perceive that effort as necessary in some other part of your life. Does it seem like a lot of work to stay in touch with your friends and family? Or does it feel like making a living is an endless, uphill battle? Or can you barely stay on top of keeping your house in order and your fridge stocked? Are you feeling exhausted or overwhelmed just *thinking* about how much you need to do for some area of your life to feel good or work well (or at all)?

Now, there are indeed many practical, healthy things you actually must do to have a life that works. But, Learned Distress can make that infinitely harder in a couple of ways. One is that Learned Distress often makes you do *more* in order to get the result you want. That could mean that it takes more energy and effort over time to eat well and exercise, or that it takes more and more energy to care for the people you love and make sure they have what they need. That increased demand is evidence that the heavy weight of Learned Distress is sitting on you, making everything harder.

The other way that Learned Distress can make feeling good so hard is a really big deal. The presence of Learned Distress largely cuts you off from the natural well-being that could propel you forward easily. As a result, you have to do two things. Depending on your survival mechanism, the first thing you must do for good things to happen is to manage your Learned Distress. If your survival mechanism keeps your Learned Distress mostly buried, you have to keep squashing it. (If you're like many of my clients, you might not even be aware of just how much energy that takes but I guarantee that it's *a lot*.) If your Learned Distress is all out in the open, you have to slog through it, go *way* around it, or put on your hiking boots to climb over a giant heap of it.

Then, once you've smashed down or gotten through/around/over your Learned Distress, you're not even done! You have to conjure energy from *somewhere* to make yourself feel good or make something good happen. You're already weary from your Learned Distress manager gig, and now you need to get ready for a house full of six-year-olds for your daughter's birthday party, or go for an hour-long run and get to the farmers' market, or finish the project your boss is hounding you about, or clean out your closet because the book you just read said it will make you happier. I know, I know, it's exhausting just thinking about it!

Managing Learned Distress *plus* manufacturing the good feelings or situations you want is exhausting and difficult. But, even if those good feelings or situations are great and therefore *seem* like they must be well-being, the level of effort and exhaustion involved with them shows us that you have been on the Learned Distress road. Your Herculean effort has paid off, and you have some good outcomes to show for it, but you're probably wondering how long you can keep that up. The good news is that you don't have to.

What Well-Being Is (and Isn't)

When your sense of self is on the well-being road, life really does feel better and easier than you have experienced before. You might feel so much more at ease with yourself that being with friends and family feels easier and less overwhelming. You might find that doing what is healthy for you happens without the kind of effort it always has taken. You might crank through your work report and get great compliments on it without it feeling difficult at all, or take your mom up on her out-of-the-blue offer to organize your daughter's birthday party for you.

But I'm not promising rainbows and unicorns. Quanta Change does not mean that you'll get to sit on the sofa all day eating ice cream and having winning lottery tickets delivered, sorry! What putting the two-year-old on the well-being road does mean is that you will get to feel good and have your life work better for you either in a way that feels easier than it has before, or perhaps, for the first time ever.

If it hasn't been clear to you before, you might discover the deep purpose for your life. Or if it has been clear to you but you still haven't been able to pursue it, you might find an opening up in the ways and means to express your uniqueness. This happened with my client who is a natural storyteller but couldn't figure out the pathway to express that aspect of herself. In a recent session, she said she had just realized how much her people's folk tales, only told orally by elders like her grandmother, meant to her. She felt a burst of inspiration to revive and record them for posterity.

One outcome I am sure of is that you will know at a deeper level than ever before that you matter just for being yourself, exactly as you are. And the people who are already in your life or new people who come into it will affirm that to you in ways you have never experienced. Like my client who said, "My husband hasn't said a kind thing to me in decades, but he looked up at me yesterday and said out of the blue, 'You are still such a beautiful woman'!" Or, my client who had resigned himself to receiving teenage spite when pushing his art-oriented daughters through their math homework. After an arduous math tutoring session, his 14-year-old stood up, threw her arms around him, and exclaimed, "Thanks, Dad! You're the best!"

How Surprisingly Effortless Well-Being Shows Up

I want to give you a couple of examples of what it's like to be in the passenger seat on the well-being road instead of trying to convince the two-year-old sense of self into swerving around the biggest potholes on the Learned Distress road.

One client's daytime shifting work was about putting her life in order. She could never make it to work on time and she struggled with hoarding. She started her next session with, "Sara, nothing happened!" (Since we're used to working hard to make good things happen, when well-being suddenly becomes the generating force, we sometimes don't notice it. Hence, "nothing happened," is the most common thing I hear at the beginning of a Quanta Change session.)

I got her talking and she said disappointedly, "I only got one part of my house cleaned out." I pressed her—how long had it been since she had cleaned out any of her house? She couldn't remember, but many years. Then, she said, "Well, I did make it to work on time every day." "Wait," I said, "really?!" She paused a moment and then said slowly, "Yeah, except for the day I got there an hour early and organized the office before everyone else came in."

We both started laughing and she was amazed, realizing how much had changed without even trying. She said if we had made a checklist with those items, she never would have accomplished it. But her well-being, unfettered for the first time by Learned Distress, propelled her through all of that without her recognizing that *anything* different had happened.

Another client was working on unlearning the most intense, universal Learned Distress: "I don't matter." She had said in the previous session, "Sara, I get that I'm going to *feel* like I matter more, but my ex-husband and his wife aren't going to treat me any differently." She started the next session by saying, "Um, I don't know what happened, but my ex-husband has never been that nice to me, and his wife just sent me a long email effusively complimenting me on how I deal with our special-needs son and asking me for advice. I didn't do or say anything different to them. I don't know how this happened, but these are miracles!"

Her story is a perfect illustration of what I say all the time—people treat you how you feel about being yourself. As she burned off a big layer of, "I don't matter," enabling the feeling, "I do matter just as I am," to expand, others started to feel that and automatically treat her better. This is the other way that the equal and opposite reaction works. The feeling you have about being yourself heads *out*, and then people respond automatically to that feeling, whatever it is. I see this happen all the time in the "I don't matter/I do matter" realm. When you feel that you don't matter, you can do everything possible to be heard—be friendly, be assertive, scream, jump up and down waving your arms—and either people don't hear you or they seem incensed that you dare to try and make yourself matter. In other words, you feel like you don't matter and that feeling comes right back at you. (Can you relate?) And then, once that shift to "I matter" happens, you don't change anything about how you communicate, and yet people hear, see, and respect you in ways you've never experienced—often the same people who were so offended before that you thought you should matter!

These are just a couple of examples of what I hear from my clients every week. These kinds of results are not unique to any of them. They are just evidence of what happens when Learned Distress is burned off and well-being takes its place.

You have natural well-being at your core, just the same as everyone else, and it's just patiently waiting there for you to uncover and experience it.

CHAPTER 7

The Quanta Change Sensory Quotient (SQ)

I'm so excited to tell you about the Quanta Change Sensory Quotient, or SQ, because it is the best way to realize that your Learned Distress is not who you really are. You are a unique expression of well-being, of feeling *good*, in the world. There are billions of unique people in the world, but only six SQ patterns—Idealist, Caregiver, Perfectionist, Optimist, Defeatist, and Dictator—that are "boxes" that Learned Distress fits into.

You may have taken personality tests before, such as Myers-Briggs or the Enneagram, that measure various traits, strengths, weaknesses, and more for the purpose of helping you navigate well through life. The SQ measures your Learned Distress and the way you survive with it, which you absorbed by the age of two and a half. The sole purpose of this personality tool is to show us your Learned Distress and survival mechanism so that you can unlearn them and uncover your natural well-being. Your SQ is graphed from a questionnaire you can fill out online, and I'll include a link to this test at the end of the book.

This personality tool was developed in Phase One of the Quanta Change research, the Humana Heart Foundation heart disease risk study. To explore her research objective, finding the source of illness, Herrmann started with the original research on stress carried out by Hans Selye, MD, PhD. While "stress" has become a somewhat vague way to describe how we react to our challenges, Selye's definition was much more specific: Stress is the *rate* of wear and tear on the body.

Herrmann focused on Selye's failure to find what *causes* that rate of wear, or in other words, what exhausts the body's ability to recover and repair. To search for the source of stress within the Humana study's research subjects, she utilized a personality tool developed by a behavioral psychologist who had studied with Selye. This scientifically validated tool focused on the way people think about themselves in response to stressors.

After analyzing the research participants' personality tool answers, Herrmann's statistician research partner revealed that this tool measured something statistically significant, asking her what that was. She named it Learned Distress, realizing that instead of measuring how people *think* about themselves, it actually measures how they *feel* about *being* themselves, namely the negative ways they feel. This led her to a wholesale reinterpretation of the tool, resulting in the SQ.

Further work with the statistician revealed the six SQ patterns. More detailed understanding of how the SQ measures the source of our non-well-being continued through research Phases Two and Three, and into my collaboration years with Herrmann when I observed and we incorporated the crucial understanding that the SQ also measures the way we survive with our negative feelings.

Your SQ Life Raft

I still recall that we were sitting at a little, round table in her living room when I told Herrmann about my lightbulb moment—that the SQ actually shows the ways we feel we *must be* to survive, in order to stay alive on the planet. That's *why* the wall of resistance to change keeps us from changing the sense of self on a rational level. It's as if it's protecting our ability to breathe. If you were to decide one day that it seemed like a good idea to dive underwater and stay there, your survival instinct would veto that right away! The SQ shows us that our sense of self holds certain ways of being, such as always doing everything perfectly or always getting everyone's approval, as being absolutely necessary to our survival, just like breathing is. So when you say, "Hey, self! I just learned that life could be easier if I don't care what people think of me, so let's go with that," your survival mechanism yells back, "Are you nuts? Getting everyone to like you is what keeps you alive! Motion denied!"

You might read through some of the SQ descriptions and think, "Why would anyone think *that's* a good way to survive? That seems crazy!" But these survival mechanisms are absorbed before the age of two and a half, before you had any rational thinking capacity, and therefore, often don't make any rational sense at all. This is why so many people have told me that understanding their SQ has helped them understand for the very first time why their lives have unfolded as they have—especially with regards to the struggles they've faced.

But you might be thinking, "Ugh, Sara! I've spent decades learning where my negative stuff comes from. I just want to change it!" If that's you, the great news is that Quanta Change actually gets rid of your Learned Distress and survival mechanism so you can move *beyond* understanding why you feel bad to *actually feeling better*, and so you can more fully express your unique well-being in the world. But I do think that you will also learn something new through the SQ, so stick with me!

The IQ Versus the SQ

We are so used to thinking that it is our rational brain that is going to fix everything for us. Herrmann saw the limitations of our thinking brain, though. Having grown up hearing about the power of positive thinking, she wondered why it wasn't actually working for everyone she saw around her. I know that some of you are saying, "Yes, I've known this was true for so long!"

Her education and work showed her that, in fact, all of our rational intelligence and thinking was only giving us ways to cope with, control, or avoid experiencing our Learned Distress and its consequences. She saw the false idea that our thinking brain could bring about a good life for us, as embodied in our embrace of the Intelligence Quotient, or IQ, as the holy grail of humanity.

As she developed and analyzed the Sensory Quotient, it became apparent that it is how we *feel*, not how we think, that is generating our lives for us. And so, if we wanted to make fundamental changes in how our lives feel and work, we would need to change on that deep feeling level. To recognize this important understanding of how life works, she named this personality tool the SQ to contrast it with the old gold standard, the IQ.

The SQ Pressure Cooker

Before I dive into the specific patterns, it's important to explain a fundamental distinction within the SQ. It measures two types of Learned Distress—one is that which you bury or deny (or at least try to keep buried most of the time) in order to survive, and the other is that which you often feel or are immersed in. Some of the six patterns are made up of nearly all one or the other, while some are a combination of both types.

You can think of your sense of self, which contains how you feel about being yourself, like a pressure cooker. You probably know that a pressure cooker relies on a tightly fitting lid so that pressure can build up in the pot to help cook the food. From the outside, it looks calm and collected, right? But inside it's a hot, boiling mess! Yup, that's right, I'm saying Learned Distress makes your sense of self a hot, boiling mess, whether you're aware of it or not.

Your SQ pattern determines how tightly your sense of self lid fits, which is one important aspect of your survival mechanism. Your perception and experience of life are determined by what you would see just walking into the kitchen. The tight-lidded patterns keep the hot, boiling mess largely hidden from you—this is the buried or denied Learned Distress. I recall a friend with a tight-lidded pattern once saying to me, "Oh, Sara, I understand what Learned Distress is. I just don't have any!" The leaky-lidded patterns continually have hot mess bubbling out, wreaking a kind of havoc or misery. So much so, that some of those folks would swear that their lid blew off entirely years ago! This, of course, is the Learned Distress you feel or are immersed in.

As I go through the specific patterns, I'll refer to them being tight-lidded or leaky-lidded. And I'll share how the tight-lidded patterns experience life when the lid starts to leak—when the intensity of Learned Distress grows to a point where the lid can't contain it anymore.

Learned Distress Versus Well-Being: Your Pattern's Treadmill Style

I have a question for you. The sun does a lot of good for us. It gives us light, heat, and energy. It enables our plants and crops to grow. It drives the weather patterns that bring about so much good for us. How hard do you have to work for all those benefits? Not one little bit, right? The sun does all of that without any effort on your part. The sun is like your well-being.

Learned Distress shuts you into a room and seals out all the sunlight. But you still need all the functions of the sun, right? Learned Distress has you covered! It puts a light in the ceiling that conveys all the basic benefits of sunlight. But there's a catch. The light is hooked up to a treadmill on which you have to run constantly to keep the light turned on. And your SQ pattern dictates how the treadmill-running goes for you. For some patterns, as long as they run the way they should, everything generally works pretty well, whereas, for other patterns, something is always going wrong on the treadmill.

Quanta Change is *not* about learning to run better! It's about getting off the treadmill and getting outside, where your well-being can work for you the way it's meant to and you can focus on expressing your uniqueness in the world. Take a moment to imagine the difference between constantly running and basking in the sun. It's one of the best ways I've found to describe how this deep shift of Quanta Change actually feels. Relaxing in the sunlight of your well-being is the result you can look forward to!

Seeing Others Through the SQ Lens

Even if you find yourself in the descriptions right away, I encourage you to read through all of them. You might find yourself saying, "Oh! That's why my boss is always cutting people off in meetings," or "No wonder my sister is constantly offering everyone something to eat!" While my goal is helping you feel better with the Quanta Change process, another great benefit for me of this work has been to understand why other people behave the way they do, especially when their behavior is very different from my own.

Specifically, the SQ helps us see that when someone is behaving badly, it's coming from their fear that something is wrong with them. In fact, I find it really helps sometimes to say to myself, "Oh, they're just scared!" (To be clear, this understanding never negates someone's responsibility for their bad behavior, though.) Each pattern brings about kneejerk survival mechanisms that can be so different from our own that we can feel like that person is from a different planet.

When I am scared, my primary SQ pattern, the Caregiver, triggers me to please, appease, and take care of everyone around me. I get small, and my own needs and opinions disappear—I can't even perceive them. I become hyperaware of what anyone else might need and try to take care of them. Fortunately, my own Quanta Change work has turned down the intensity of this reaction to an occasional two or three, instead of nearly constant 10 or 11 like it used to be.

When someone with the pattern exactly opposite mine on the SQ, the Dictator, panics, their kneejerk reaction is exactly opposite. I once saw a friend and fellow Quanta Change participant completely and inappropriately take over in a situation that was not his to run. I was flabbergasted and asked what he thought he was doing! He said, "Oh, yeah, when I get scared, I take over. It happens before I even realize it." I'm still a little shocked because it would be the very last thing I would ever do.

I am guessing that when you read through the six pattern descriptions, you'll find equally surprising survival mechanisms, along with one or more that describes you to a T. (It's possible to have a combination of a couple or even three SQ patterns.) So, let's dive into them!

CHAPTER 8

The Idealist SQ Pattern

If you have this pattern, you survive by trying to make your life into your ideal, and you often succeed for a great deal of time. It can be an across-the-board ideal way of being—in your relationships, how you present yourself in the world, in your health, in your career, and how you move through daily life. Or you might focus in on making some particular part of life the way it "should" be, whatever that means for you. For instance, creating the ideal family or career could consume most of your life.

"Should" is the first word that comes to me when I think of the Idealist pattern, and you might find yourself saying it a lot. The Idealist pattern tells you that if you make your life match the ideal picture in your head, if you make it the way it should be, you can feel good and life can work well for you. Often, Idealists then feel that they can't let anyone see when something in their life doesn't conform to their ideal, and they can feel embarrassed if someone does see behind that curtain.

This survival pressure to make everything ideal can extend beyond your own personal bubble. You might find that you attempt to make your family members' or friends' lives the way you feel they should be. This probably just seems to you like the caring thing to do, to make sure the people you love are well and their lives are working well. But you might also feel the pressure to *fix* everything and everyone around you all the time. Sometimes, if you really think about it for a moment, you might realize that you feel that you need to fix the entire world. That is some serious survival pressure!

Pressure Cooker Type: Tight Lid

For Idealists, survival depends on keeping Learned Distress buried. This isn't just about denial—this pattern often keeps Learned Distress hidden even from you. I'll never forget an Idealist who said to me, "I understand what Learned Distress is, Sara. I just don't have any!" And yet you didn't have to talk to her for very long before you could hear the effects of Learned Distress in her life. Idealists feel an internal pressure to have a life about which they can say, "Everything is great!" You can see how feeling that there's something wrong with you could get in the way of that!

One way to keep Learned Distress under control is to stay super busy. If you never stop going, there won't be time to feel all those icky feelings. You might find yourself saying what many clients have said: "When something feels bad, I just keep moving. I don't want to get stuck in the negative." You might employ self-help methods like gratitude journaling or affirmations to outrun negative feelings when they pop up. You could think of this as clamping the lid back on tightly when a little bit of the Learned Distress hot mess finds a way to splatter out for a moment.

Treadmill-Running Style: Idealists run constantly and often beautifully. And they usually take great pains to keep the treadmill in fine working order. That keeps them busy, of course, and busy equals no time to feel Learned Distress! It's also the way treadmill owners *should* behave, right?

Idealist Pattern Breakdown

Each of the six survival mechanisms breaks down when Learned Distress overwhelms the mechanism's ability to contain or cope with it, and it's where you start to realize that the way you've been surviving just doesn't work in some way.

For Idealists, that rising Learned Distress intensity starts to mess with your ability to keep the lid clamped down. One way you might have experienced this is to be frustrated that despite making all the parts of your life the way they should be, you're still not feeling good—or you're even feeling worse over time. The promise of the Idealist pattern hasn't paid off, and you might even beat yourself up for not feeling good like you think you should. Or you might be thinking, "I've done *everything* the way I should and it hasn't paid off. No fair!" (Agreed! But Learned Distress never plays fair, unfortunately.)

Or you might be working harder and harder just to get the same results—or those results stop happening, despite doing things the ideal way that has always worked for you before. This can be especially painful if some part of the ideal picture falls apart in a way that others can see. For a number of my clients, divorce is the biggest example, and it has been devastating for them to feel they have failed in this way. Other examples might include losing your job, getting sick more often, or having a child who struggles in a way that seems to prove you haven't been the ideal parent. Again, the Idealist *pattern* (remember, this isn't who you really are) will often demand that the people around you conform to your ideal also.

You might have felt like this breakdown started to happen at some earlier point in your life but then you found a way to get back on the right track. The Idealist pattern can be very resourceful in clamping the lid back on or in getting your treadmill back in working order, so you can get back to running. You might have even gotten through a major life trauma, like a divorce or a big health crisis, but you felt like you were past it and could resume saying, "Everything is great!"

But—and I take no joy in saying this—Learned Distress is like water filling up a reservoir behind a dam, and the rains keep coming. The rising intensity of Learned Distress will eventually overwhelm your ability to keep it under control, and when that happens you might feel like life is spinning out of control. And you might feel shocked because your survival mechanism had hidden all of those awful feelings and their outcomes from you.

From Idealist Pattern to Well-Being

The number one change I see happen for Idealists is that life gets *easier*. I've so often heard something like this: "I usually do a lot of preparation for a meeting, but I just spent a few minutes on it and it was a great success. I just walked in with everything I already know and it went better than I could have imagined, with so much less effort. Just being myself was enough!"

Sometimes this greater ease can show up as being able to work within your own capacity, instead of miles beyond it. One client said,

"I would set my own deadline that was far in advance of my client's expectation, and then feel the pressure to meet it." Her ability to do this to herself was eliminated by a severe, chronic illness, but even though she couldn't meet the internal deadline anymore, she felt very guilty about it. Once she'd peeled away some of that Learned Distress, she no longer felt the need to push beyond capacity *and* she doesn't feel guilty about it. Another related example was the client who said, "I'm able to actually *enjoy* nature while sitting out on my deck now, instead of that just being a momentary, guilt-ridden break from my long to-do list." Quanta Change allows Idealists to actually do what is best for them and what feels good, rather than having to tirelessly work toward the ideal.

In order to fulfill the ideal picture, people with this pattern usually feel a strong need to know what that picture should look like, so they can figure out how they'll make it all happen—like feeling pressured to mentally put a jigsaw puzzle together when the pieces are all still sitting in a pile. Maybe you're enthusiastically nodding yes right now? One of my clients started describing her changes as the "flexibility to be messy." It started small—the ability to not need "everything in place and perfect right now!" in her home. She could leave crumbs on the kitchen counter for a while and not be jumping out of her skin, for instance. But that flexibility quickly extended to taking on a new business venture without being able to see how every little bit of it was going to work out. She said before Quanta Change, she probably would have walked away from that opportunity because she couldn't yet see exactly how it would all work out.

The Idealist pattern can make it painful or embarrassing to share anything that isn't "great" with others. Many clients have found that they can relax and openly express more of who they really are with others without feeling uncomfortable in that old, familiar way. And, as I say all the time, other people treat us the way *we feel* about being ourselves. So, when you feel comfortable sharing more of your real self, you are met by people seeing you and welcoming your uniqueness.

One very common piece of Learned Distress is not feeling safe, which ultimately boils down to the feeling that "I don't matter." That's because being harmed by others is a negation of our right to exist and be well. Often, people will feel unsafe in multiple ways. For instance, one of my clients didn't feel safe walking out to her mailbox in the dark, despite living in a resort town with very little crime. When she did need to step outside briefly at night, she would do so with hyper-vigilance—her body tensed, her heart pounding, and her eyes darting around to be sure that no one was lurking in the darkness. She traced this back to growing up on the edge of a major city, hearing about crime from her parents and the news. She also didn't feel emotionally safe with others, especially men, and she saw a pattern of being lied to and abused by men in both romantic and other relationships. This stemmed from being sexually abused by her father.

As she peeled off layers of Learned Distress around not being safe, she first felt safe enough to walk out to her mailbox at night and then eventually to calmly walk around a bit by herself in her town after dark. She also has experienced greater safety in relationships with others. It started with being able to be more open, direct, and real with women in ways that brought about a good, safe outcome for her. And then, she was able to more comfortably express what she really thought and felt with men. A man she wasn't interested in asked her out on a date, and she was honest and direct in telling him she wasn't interested in him that way. She said it felt so much safer than anything like this she'd ever done before. And she's even feeling safe enough that she's started to get to know a new man with the potential of it becoming a romantic relationship, after years of wondering if she would ever feel comfortable considering that again.

As I said before, this survival mechanism can demand that the people around you conform to the ideal also. So, Idealists often find themselves trying to help the people close to them do just that. Are you exhausted thinking about ways you've done that? One client has spent her whole life doing that, and by her late 60s, the constant work of dealing with a now-adult special needs child had really taken its toll. As she removed Learned Distress, she found herself able to wait before jumping in to rescue him. To her amazement, she found that very often, he would step up in ways he never had before, or resources to help him showed up so that the burden of his care didn't always have to fall on her. Of course, she still provides what she needs to and steps in when necessary. But, for the first time in her life, what matters to her is at the center of her life, and she's able to take really good care of herself first. And, I'll add, without the crushing guilt that this pattern so often uses as leverage to keep you toiling away for the ideal.

CHAPTER 9

The Defeatist SQ Pattern

This pattern demands that you prove nothing works for you in order to survive. Wait, you're thinking, "How can that possibly be a survival mechanism?!" I know it sounds counterintuitive, especially if you don't have this pattern. And, even if you do have this pattern, you might feel a strange confusion within yourself between the pressure to prove that nothing works and your rational understanding that this isn't helpful!

There are two main functions of this survival mechanism that happen automatically and persistently. One is what younger clients describe as a lack of will to do what they should and anyone over the age of 25 describes as a sensation of being held or dragged backward while they are trying to move forward. This can prevent the Defeatist from doing the things they know would be beneficial for them or even crucial to their life working well. As a result, people with this pattern are often accused of, or even beat themselves up for, engaging in self-sabotage. But it's not conscious or deliberate. This is just evidence of the equal and opposite reaction generating another familiar situation in which nothing works; no one chooses to feel lousy or act in self-defeating ways.

The second function is a phenomenon of failing despite all efforts to succeed. If I give an Idealist and a Defeatist the same task, the Defeatist will invariably work twice as hard and perform it more meticulously than the Idealist, and yet the Idealist will be a brilliant success while the Defeatist is left out in the cold. The first two friends I accurately identified as Defeatists are extraordinary in their fields and were both pursuing doctorates. And yet they continually experienced failure where they should have succeeded.

Another way you might have experienced this is that you are always really nice, terribly accommodating, unwaveringly thoughtful toward others. And yet you never get the payoff of being treated like you matter. You never get the reward of a good, lasting relationship that benefits you.

Because of these limiting functions, you might get to a point in life where you wonder what the point of continuing to struggle to succeed is, and you can start to give up. You may always feel like you're waiting for the other shoe to drop. People around you are probably saying that you should just stop being so negative. But what I know is that you're just expressing the way life is for you. It's an infuriating way to try to survive. And if you've recognized yourself here, I know you're all too well aware.

Pressure Cooker Type: Leaky Lid

"Lid? What lid, Sara?! That hot, boiling mess has been splattering and spilling out all over the place as long as I can remember." I know. You've been feeling your Learned Distress forever, and no matter what you've done, you've just continued to feel worse. Maybe there's some part of your life where it's especially apparent. Perhaps you have struggled to have or hold onto relationships, either in your personal or professional life, like my client whose first Quanta Change goal was to have a friendship that, for once, lasted more than a couple of years. Perhaps you've had big health challenges that you can't find a way to solve. Maybe you are a top achiever in your career field but you never reap the benefits in terms of recognition, income, or stability. Maybe you identify with my clients who have said they have no power over their own lives but are just at the mercy of a seemingly mysterious force always pulling them in the wrong direction.

Treadmill-Running Style: "It's hard to run when my knees are always injured or the machine is falling apart, Sara!" Again, I hear you. Defeatists are continually trying to overcome some challenge to moving forward in life, and often, they just can't.

Defeatist SQ Pattern Breakdown

For this pattern, it's more of the same, but intensifies over time. You might find yourself more overwhelmed or exasperated by things not working out well. Situations in which you've held things together through sheer will finally fall apart. People who have stuck with you for a long time might abandon you, citing your negativity as the reason.

You can also start to feel a strange, inner tug-of-war. The need to prove that nothing ever works keeps getting stronger. But as you move through life, the well-being at your core increasingly demands to be heard. Not to mention, the need for things to work out well just so you can function begins to scream at you. Because I have a bit of this pattern in my own SQ, I know this struggle. On one hand, you desperately want to succeed. On the other, this strong inner force is dragging you back, and part of you might even feel celebratory when some failure occurs. If you have felt this, you're not alone. It really is just a function of the well-being part of you wanting to win out over that dastardly Defeatist Learned Distress.

From Defeatist to Well-Being

Yes, if you're a Defeatist, that internal voice might be yelling, "But nothing ever works for me so this probably won't either!" But everything below comes straight from people just like you, and if it worked for them, it can work for you!

I get so excited when a Defeatist client starts talking about what they actually like or want in life. If you have this pattern, it can be scary to let yourself want good things for yourself. It feels really risky to hope for something when you're pretty sure it's not going to happen, right? One client has talked so often about not even knowing or being able to express what he wants, which has been a huge frustration for his spouse. His survival mechanism had completely suppressed the desire for what mattered to him because what was even the point? As Learned Distress peeled away, he started to remember or discover new things that he really loves doing. And he's been able to start talking with his wife about how he really feels and what he really wants. They've had more meaningful conversations, he's experiencing less of her exasperation at his noncommunication, and he's feeling more and more like he can be himself with her. As a result, he feels like he matters more to her. Wanting to feel good and have what you really want is a function of the well-being that

The Defeatist SQ Pattern

fits under the big "I matter" umbrella, which is the foundation of good relationships, and so when people with the Defeatist pattern uncover well-being in this vein, they are able to start connecting better with others and their relationships vastly improve.

Another example in this "I matter" vein is a client who has started to evaluate to-do list items based on whether they will benefit her or not. Before this, her needs and wants always came last, if they even made it on the list. And if she tried to sort her list on this new basis, she felt crushing guilt and abandoned the effort. She's still seeing to the practicalities and actual needs of her family and coworkers, but all the time she used to spend on things she hated is now going to activities she loves. She's learning a new instrument and picking up craft projects she had left behind long ago.

That Defeatist "held or dragged back" feeling is a great one to see ease up, too. A client who has experienced tons of that was just telling me how he's found himself taking lots of action toward his retirement goals. He'd gotten to the point of not really being able to do that at all, or at least not without dread and Herculean effort. But he said these recent efforts have felt energizing and even fun.

Another typical Defeatist characteristic is the inability to accept compliments or congratulations on something that went well. If you have this survival mechanism, you already know that your knee-jerk reaction to such a statement starts with, "Yeah, but . . . ." Am I right? You can always find something, probably several things, that were still not good enough or haven't worked out. Always feeling like you have to do things more and more perfectly is a hallmark of this pattern, and that voice is only too happy to contradict anyone who has the audacity to say something good about you. So, starting to feel like you are good enough just as you are, and then actually accept it when someone notices that, is a big sign of Quanta Change happening. The next-level change here is being willing to volunteer something good yourself. I always know that a Defeatist client has peeled off a big Learned Distress layer when they lead off in our phone session with a *great* thing that happened that week.

CHAPTER 10

The Perfectionist SQ Pattern

This survival mechanism is not typically what you would think of when you hear that word; namely, obsessing over having everything in order or doing things perfectly, although you might feel that way if you have this pattern. The Perfectionist pattern demands you to keep everything under control or within tight boundaries in order for you to survive. Or you might relate more to the idea that there is a right or correct or prudent way of doing things that you need to conform to, and that way is the *only* way to do things.

If you have this pattern, you might feel uncomfortable or even unsafe if anyone around you steps over your boundaries, or if their behavior is outside the boundaries of what is right for you. For instance, one client's boundaries required that other people asked before they did anything for her, even something like washing the dishes, and so gestures by others that some people might find thoughtful actually felt threatening to her. This *tight boundaries* aspect of the Perfectionist pattern can lead to feeling overwhelmed by other people pretty often. You might feel like you need to put some kind of protection around yourself when going into spaces with lots of people, for instance. Or you might find yourself strongly feeling like someone else just needs to get themselves under control *now*.

You may have the sense that something is just "too much" for you. It might be that you need to carefully control your schedule, your environment, your social media use, or some other aspect of life in order to keep your boundaries from being overrun. For instance, one of my clients feels that driving to the next (connected) town over feels like too much to handle on any kind of regular basis.

Or you might feel like you need to keep your own self and behavior within tight boundaries. It will likely feel to you as though this is just what is right, responsible, ethical, or practical. This could be with regards to your feelings, your interactions with others, how you eat and exercise, how you keep your house, how you take care of your pets, or pretty much any aspect of life.

Pressure Cooker Type: Tight Lid

Of all the patterns, this is perhaps the most tightly lidded survival mechanism. Survival means keeping all of your negative stuff under control. That's the really interesting thing about this pattern. You feel that by creating strong boundaries, you're keeping all the stuff that's wrong for you *outside* of you. What you're actually doing is keeping your Learned Distress deeply buried *inside* of you. But often when I start working with Perfectionists, their Learned Distress is so hidden from them that they're genuinely not aware of having their negative feelings buried. From the outside, your pressure cooker looks shiny and calm. What I know after two decades of helping

Perfectionists feel better is that inside there's a hot, boiling mess for you, just like everyone else. If that feels scary to contemplate, what I want you to know is that getting rid of that messy Learned Distress is *safe* and that freeing up your well-being will allow you to feel so much better than your strong boundaries ever have.

Treadmill-Running Style: You run safely, carefully, and in a controlled and prudent manner. You have the right kind of shoes and socks. You don't tend to draw attention to yourself. Staying under people's radar is generally the safest way to be. You do all the recommended treadmill maintenance right on time because to do anything else would be stupid.

Perfectionist SQ Pattern Breakdown

The breakdown for all the survival mechanisms happens when the rising intensity of Learned Distress overwhelms your control mechanisms for it—when it overcomes your pressure cooker lid's ability to keep it sealed away. Much as with the Idealist pattern, if you have the Perfectionist pattern, you probably have experienced episodes of lid-seal failure in the past, when something felt more intense to you than was comfortable, when things weren't working the right way despite your very best efforts, when you felt like your ability to keep things under control or your ability to maintain your boundaries was blown. Like Idealists, you probably were able to get things pretty quickly back to your normal state.

But you might also feel like those episodes have happened more often, or even like you're not able to really get things on the right track again. You might be saying what clients often say to me, one of whom put it this way: "I've done *everything* right and it's not working!" Feeling that things are out of control or off track in some way is the number one reason Perfectionists start Quanta Change. This could be an internal experience of experiencing your negative emotions at a level that is no longer tolerable. Or it could be your health, your relationships, your work, or some aspect of your daily life that has begun to press against your comfortable boundaries. One client said that she felt more and more often like screaming, "I just can't handle it!"

For many, a battle takes place as this survival mechanism breaks down. The natural consequence of this pattern's demand for you to stay under control can make you invisible. You might struggle to be seen or heard. I liken this to living deep within a fortress in order to stay safe and keep the wrong people and experiences out. You do stay safe, but it's impossible to connect with others through all those thick stone walls. Others can't even see that you're there, much less connect with you. As a result, sometimes Perfectionists start to feel increasingly that they don't matter, that they can't get seen or heard. The most fundamental need we have as human beings is to matter. So, the well-being based need to matter and the survival mechanism based need to live in the fortress to stay safe collide.

Living inside the fortress, believe it or not, can even keep you hidden from yourself. What I mean by that is that you might have a hard time connecting to what really matters to you, to who you really are, to what you really want, or to your purpose in life. Being confused or in the dark about your direction in life or what you want in some way can be a clue that this survival mechanism is starting to really get in the way of your ability to feel good.

From Perfectionist to Well-Being

A greater feeling of ease and safety in just being themselves is probably the first thing I hear from Perfectionists, and that continues to increase over time. One client said that she didn't even realize she wasn't giving herself the freedom to be authentic. She told me about a lunch with a longtime friend who often dominated their conversations. She'd peeled away some Learned Distress layers by this point, and she found herself sharing more freely with this friend than she had in the past, tiptoeing less around things that felt like they might harm the relationship. Not only did she feel more comfortable than she had before, but their conversation was more equal than in the past. They both enjoyed the interaction, and my client said she felt like there was more space for her.

Around the same time, this client also found herself rearranging the art in her home, which in the past brought about anxiety in doing it the right way. But now, the activity felt freer, like finger painting, she said. It was just fun. She also started poking around into a new job search, instead of holding off for a more "right" time. Well-being allows you to do things in your own unique way, in your own space and time, instead of being boxed into some "right" way.

Another great example was a client who had described her very careful eating habits to me in detail over time. She was experiencing some health issues that treatments weren't helping her overcome. As she removed layers of Perfectionist Learned Distress, she found herself craving foods she hadn't eaten in a long time, that had felt outside her "right way" of eating. (Not chocolate cake for breakfast! Things like adding in fish and certain vegetables.) She started to be able to hear what her body was asking for, and as she incorporated some of these foods back into her diet, she felt much better. Isn't it interesting how her Perfectionist tight boundaries were preventing her from her own intuitive sense of what was actually good for her, but that once the Learned Distress was gone she effortlessly knew what her body needed?

One Perfectionist client used to dread going to a conference each year with the same group of people because of the fear of being overwhelmed by others, even people she liked. But the more Learned Distress layers she peeled off, the more she looked forward to and really enjoyed those conferences for the social time in them. Even I was surprised when she called me after one of those conferences, nearly gushing about what a great time she had. She sounded like a different person. She also found that people were seeing her and noticing her in ways that felt good and safe to her. This can be a shocking but great change for Perfectionists, who have only felt safe when hidden safely away inside the fortress.

The boundaries we create to control some aspect or outcome of Learned Distress must be carefully maintained, and as Learned Distress intensity rises, boundary maintenance takes more and more effort. But well-being actually creates *natural* boundaries that allow us to simply be ourselves without all of that extra protection work. Clients sometimes see this as their well-being radiating effortlessly and freely outward from themselves, instead of having to maintain the fortress walls.

CHAPTER 11

The Optimist SQ Pattern

This is another pattern where the name of it isn't what you would consider it to mean. I think of this one as "all crisis all the time." In order to prove that tomorrow will be better, this survival mechanism demands that you have a crisis *today*. The problem is that your sense of self that stores your survival mechanism only understands the *present* moment. So, that future good is eternally in the *future*, and you're stuck in present crisis after present crisis. You just overcome one only to be thrust into the next one. Or if you're an Optimist, you might experience this as constant, ongoing struggle.

This continual crisis cycle is something others might often label as "drama," and they might even assume or suggest that you are perpetuating it in some conscious way. But, one more time, no one *chooses* to be miserable or in a crisis. An Optimist's constant struggle is simply the Learned Distress road their two-year-old sense of self keeps driving down.

You might be aware of your survival mechanism's perpetual search for the next crisis. You might encounter some little challenge and hear a weird voice in your head say, "Yeah, I could make something *big* out of this!" You might be aware that such a struggle, while not something you would *prefer*, is a comfort zone for you. The thought of things being easier or smoother might even make you feel uneasy.

You might feel like you're in a tug-of-war. On one hand, you feel pressure to prove to yourself and others that you're overcoming the current crisis and that things are *going* to be good, even if you feel lousy right now. On the other hand, you're very aware of, even feel immersed in, your Learned Distress. You are probably no stranger to most of the big "flavors" of Learned Distress—I don't matter, I don't fit, I can't be healthy easily, I can't succeed easily, I'm never good enough, I have to work for people's approval. And yet you yearn to overcome these awful feelings, so you might feel pulled in both directions all the time.

Pressure Cooker Type: Leaky Lid

I already gave it away, but you would have guessed it anyhow, right? This pattern immerses you in your Learned Distress, and like the Defeatists, you might be thinking, "Lid? What lid?! Just look at everything splattered all over the stovetop despite my constant cleaning efforts!"

Treadmill-Running Style: Running and keeping the machine in working order is a constant struggle. You keep things moving ahead, and you probably smile much of the time you're doing it, but it is a *lot* of work.

Optimist Pattern Breakdown

Again, much like the Defeatist pattern, when your Learned Distress starts to overcome your survival mechanism, it probably feels like more of the same, but a *lot* more. Your struggles might start to be so big you wonder if you can continue to overcome them. You might start to wonder if things really will ever get better. Your struggles start to become more exhausting and exasperating instead of motivating and weirdly comforting. The new tug-of-war is between your survival mechanism's demand for more crisis and your desire to actually feel good and have your life work well *now*. People may get more frustrated by your constant crisis, and some of them may even walk away from you as a result.

From Optimist to Well-Being

As you peel away Learned Distress, as the intensity of it is lessened, you'll see a corresponding drop in the intensity of your struggles. You might see the same kinds of crises happen for a while, but if you think back and measure them against past events, you'll find that they aren't as big and don't deliver the same emotional punch. Much like people with the Idealist pattern, with whom you share the drive to always make good things happen, you will likely find that successes start to become *easier* to achieve.

As the need for crisis calms down, you start to become comfortable with calm and peace. This may feel really strange at first, because it's so different from "all crisis all the time." One Optimist client started leaving work crisis behind at the end of her day instead of staying at her job and slogging through more of it. She started to let other people take on more of the burden of their group's work, and instead of that triggering a new crisis, it worked great and she felt better.

One client experienced a lot of struggles with her family. Relationship issues will always come back to the biggest fundamental piece of Learned Distress you share with all of humanity—the feeling that you don't matter. Leaky-lidded Optimists, of course, feel immersed in that feeling, and at the same time feel like they must *make* themselves matter. She was in constant motion trying to do that with her family. She traveled a lot to see family, and when she did, she often struggled with them to get things to happen in ways that allowed her to feel that she mattered, meaning that she was seen, heard, and valued for being herself. She worked especially hard in her relationship with her father, who seemed especially resistant to showing her that she mattered!

As she peeled off Learned Distress layers, she didn't feel she needed to try so hard with her family. This showed us already that she was feeling more of the well-being that she matters just for being herself, not for being the person who makes family gatherings happen a certain way. She also found that she didn't *have* to make things work with her difficult brother if he simply wasn't going to meet her halfway. And her changes in relating to her father have been the biggest. She's found new ways to connect with him that work better—that work great, even—and her internal push to make their relationship fit her hoped-for picture has calmed way down. He's even started communicating more with her on his own instead of only in response to her (often frustrated) reaching out. Relationship successes always confirm what I say often: People treat you the way you feel about being yourself. If you feel like you don't matter and you have to struggle to make yourself matter, others' responses to your efforts will be, "Nice try, but you don't matter. Try harder!" Whereas when you, like this client, uncover a lot of your "I matter" well-being, others will automatically treat you like you matter more and more.

Another Optimist's crisis was with her career and family. She and her husband both are senior-level faculty in the same small niche of academia, and they had failed for years to find jobs at the same university. This wasn't for a lack of trying. Both had applied at the other's school, going through intensive interview processes with their spouse's close colleagues, always ending up with being turned down. Talk about an awkward next day at the office! They were living two hours apart in a part of the country with intense winter weather, commuting to be together when at all possible. During this same time, their children were born, which included a high-risk pregnancy. Their first son had big medical issues that required multiple surgeries far from their home. Aren't you exhausted just reading about it?

She finally was offered a job at her husband's school, but previously, the faculty there had made it clear that her innovative ideas weren't welcome. She risked not getting tenure there, and the thought of leaving her tenured job at a prestigious school was agonizing. Then, after she'd peeled off some giant layers of Learned Distress, she and her husband both interviewed at the same school, new to both of them. The interview process was a different universe from the experience she'd had at her husband's school. The faculty there were positive, relaxed, complimentary of her skills and ideas. She felt like she could just be herself for the first time and she said, "Wow, my opinions really do matter!" Shortly after, that school called and offered them both jobs with immediate tenure. They moved a few months later and are thriving at their new workplace, not to mention in their new home (singular!) where they finally get to raise their boys together. Unlearning big layers of the Optimist pattern's need to have continual crises allowed my client to finally experience ease and the payoff for all of her hard work. Did you just breathe a big sigh of relief like I did? Imagine living through that shift from struggle to well-being!

CHAPTER 12

The Caregiver SQ Pattern

This pattern stems from the Caregiver's feeling that they just can't do it all on their own, that they don't have it in them to rely on themselves, often in many ways. This survival mechanism demands that you create reciprocal, dependent relationships in order to make up for this inability to accomplish your goals on your own. You might not see it that way, though. You probably just feel that you are a really nice person and that you like helping others. And there's undoubtedly a permanent, well-being side to that. But, if you're a Caregiver, your survival mechanism leverages your caring superpower in order to try and overcome your perceived inadequacies.

If you have this pattern, you're probably a people-pleaser and someone who works to fit in with others. You have a good radar for knowing how to be in order to get people to like you. I'll never forget a party I threw in high school. I was so excited to have my friends over, but then I spent the entire night cooking and getting everyone food, barely speaking a word to anyone. That's because I couldn't figure out which person to be—the one I was with my parents (who were there) or the one I was with my friends at school! That's why I sometimes call this pattern the chameleon, making yourself into whomever you need to be in any given situation. You might feel that you're just being nice and agreeable, but in the end, you're really focused mostly on what you believe will make others beholden to you, or at least reciprocate with what you feel you need from them at that moment. (You might remember that this is my primary SQ pattern, so if you're cringing and yet nodding a reluctant yes right now, I can relate!)

This is because your survival depends on others' approval and support. You can usually make relationships work well and look pretty good—at least from the outside—although, this is often based on making things okay with the other person at the expense of your wants and needs. To these ends, you are probably the peacemaker in any group and you hate conflict, and yet that even extends to not being able to speak up for yourself, and you may often feel taken advantage of. (Perhaps the word "doormat" leaps to mind? Again, I can relate!)

That sense that you aren't capable within yourself has some different aspects to it. You might doubt your own ability to figure things out, to know how to do things well. This may prompt you to look to another person to tell you how to do things, and you probably feel comfortable with conforming to someone else's way. It may be that you don't even know *what* you want to do—ranging from how to spend an afternoon to who to date to what you want to do with your life. I've had several Caregiver clients who hit this particular "what now and who am I?" wall when their kids went off to college. So, again, you might be looking to others to give you direction.

All of this can add up to you being labeled "needy" by others, and you probably feel that way at times. And yet this is how it's always been for you and you have no idea how else to move through life.

Pressure Cooker Type: Combination of Tight Lid and Leaky Lid

If you're a Caregiver, you might find that the lid is pretty tightly clamped down on the personal side of your life. So, in your relationships, you have the capacity to make them work well and can often say, "Everything's great!" But then you might feel like the Learned Distress is splattering all over the place when it comes to trying to achieve your goals or in some aspect of your health.

Treadmill-Running Style: Again, you probably feel a split between the relationships part of life and the side that's about achievement and health. As long as you keep up with your treadmill maintenance and run the way anyone should, the relationships side goes pretty well. But for the other side of life, your treadmill is always falling apart or something is hampering your ability to run. And as a Caregiver, you often feel like the only way you'll succeed in your health, career, or other goals is to gain someone's help with maintenance, and you might feel like you need to get a running partner or even a coach to tell you how to run.

Caregiver SQ Pattern Breakdown

This survival mechanism breaks down when Learned Distress rises to such an intensity level that it becomes clear that your efforts to make good relationships happen (often at this point through gritted teeth) and manipulate people to help you (I'm cringing with you!)

just doesn't work. The more you try to get people to see, hear, and respond to your needs, the more invisible you feel. Perhaps people who have helped you stop. And you might start to say *that* thing: "I just give, give, give, and I never get anything back." Even if there are people you can still please by fulfilling some need of theirs, and even if people keep lending you their help, you feel at a deep level that this reciprocation isn't fulfilling the deepest human need there is, which is to matter (to be seen, heard, loved) just for being yourself.

As the reciprocation dries up (or if it really never panned out in the first place), your health or self-sufficiency challenges grow. You feel like there's no way for you to support yourself, emotionally, physically, or perhaps even financially. And yet, perhaps for the first time, you're forced into fending for yourself in these ways. Those people you've so carefully cultivated relationships with in order to try and meet your needs might abandon you because of your increasing neediness. I can speak from personal experience that this can be deeply painful and scary. You're not alone!

From Caregiver to Well-Being

The shift to well-being for you, if you're a Caregiver, is toward greater empowerment from within. That's true of all the patterns in different ways, but it's more obvious and clear-cut for Caregivers because you have felt such an absence of it. You will uncover the well-being that allows you to know how to handle things on your own and the well-being strength to do just that. You will find that you know what's right for you, instead of depending on others to tell you what you should think and do.

You'll uncover the fundamentally important aspect of well-being, that you matter just for being yourself. You will be increasingly centered on your well-being and how good it feels to be you, and you will care less and less what other people think of you! (I know, I know, it sounds so far-fetched, but I can speak from personal experience that it's true!) Because people treat you how you feel about being yourself, the more you feel that you matter, the more people will see and hear you, and they will be more willing to accommodate your needs, instead of it always being the other way around.

One of my clients had been the textbook Caregiver both at home and at work, as a registered nurse who homeschooled her kids and took care of her mom through a long illness at the end of her life. Once she became inexplicably ill herself, she could no longer "give, give, give," and was forced to admit that her survival mechanism didn't work. (This kind of physical breakdown can be the Learned Distress dam breaking in any of the six patterns.) But, as she unlearned layers of Caregiver Learned Distress, she started telling her family and friends what she actually wanted and needed, like ending an evening gathering early so she could go to bed. Much to her surprise, no one minded! I see these changes for people all the time but even I was surprised the day this mild-mannered woman said, "Dammit, I do matter!" And she continued to see more and more the well-being reciprocation of her feeling that—her family honoring her needs, her ways of doing things (like discontinuing big holiday decorating and meals), and at long last, putting her first in ways that should have been all the way along. She finally got to live her own life instead of taking care of everyone else's.

Another client saw a lot of her shifts happen at work. As a teacher, she was always accommodating everyone else in her school. Their needs always came first, and she started to feel hurt and resentful that she wasn't getting what she needed. As she peeled away Caregiver Learned Distress, she started being recognized for everything she was doing. Her principal said, "You're really a leader here," which was nothing she'd ever heard before. She was asked by a vice superintendent to be an official mentor of new teachers because she's so good at it. She said she finally felt valued in the way she'd always wanted to be. One day, she said about some divvying up of school resources, "I'm going to take my piece of the pie and not feel bad about it." Caregivers often feel very uncomfortable with anything that could be characterized as "winning," so this was a big breakthrough. In this same vein, she found herself no longer taking all of the responsibility for situations that involved difficult students or colleagues, whereas she'd usually done the typical Caregiver thing of feeling that it was all her fault.

She started to trust and value her own knowledge and gifts more. She started coming up with her own creative solutions for difficult students and they worked great. Every time she'd hear a teacher talking about some new lesson rubric or system, she had always had a typical Caregiver response of, "Oh, no! Another set of guidelines that I have to learn!" But she realized that a lot of these systems were there for the purpose of bringing about the kind of teaching she had always done instinctively. She was *already* good enough just being herself! Out of the blue, she didn't acquiesce to a dictatorial teacher to whom she'd always subordinated herself. She stopped second-guessing her skills or judgment. In less than a year, she went from dreading the next school year to finding the love she originally had for teaching.

Another client saw a great deal of progress in a very typical Caregiver scenario, which is a complete focus on finding a romantic partner almost to the exclusion of anything else. She was recovering from a painful breakup but already trying to figure out how she could shift herself to find the right partner. Within a few months, she started to see that security and fulfillment were something that came from within, not from a partner. Her focus shifted to how she wanted her career to move forward instead. She also started to really enjoy her time to herself instead of going out to clubs with people she didn't even find that interesting. She said, "For the first time in my life, I'm not lonely." She'd learned a lot *about* self-care, but she actually started to enjoy *doing* things she loves, like spending time outdoors and diving into creative projects. Caregivers are always focused on everyone else, so self-care rarely is a real option for them. She also started to choose what to do with her time based on what she wanted, indicating that she had uncovered a great deal of "I matter" well-being. Instead of dropping everything to get together with friends, she'd say, "I have this project I want to finish. I could meet up with you in a couple of hours."

CHAPTER 13

The (Benevolent) Dictator Pattern

While I generally use Dictator alone to name this pattern, you can assume that "benevolent" is implied. As people with all of the survival mechanisms are doing, Dictators are not only doing their very best despite their Learned Distress, but they often see what they are doing as being for other people's good.

As you read through this description, though, you may notice that its characteristics line up with traits of people who act in dark or harmful ways toward others personally or from positions of power. They are at the far end of the Dictator spectrum, and as I said earlier, understanding that someone's actions stem from Learned Distress never negates their culpability for their actions.

This survival mechanism demands that you establish your way as the only way and that you make sure that the situations in your life conform to that way. You often extend this to telling others that you know what's best for them. And "dictating" your vision might be the primary or only way you feel able to connect with others. You might find it difficult to connect on a more personal level and form good relationships, and then, in your desire for connection, you may overpower others. (This could still be in ways you and even they feel are benevolent.)

You are probably very smart and you achieve goals easily, which likely includes the goal of maintaining good health. You might feel strongly that you need to show others how much you know, and you might even pretend you know things you don't.

You are probably competitive and this likely relates to everything from where you and a friend go for lunch up to making sure you always have the upper hand at work. If you feel uneasy in a situation with others, you may tend to overcome that by becoming the dominant voice in the room. You might find yourself frequently opposing someone else's opinions in a kneejerk way, sometimes even when you recently stated their same view. It's possible that these characteristics have caused you to clash with authority throughout your life.

Pressure Cooker Type:
Combination of Tight Lid and Leaky Lid

In the realms of achieving goals and health, you can probably keep Learned Distress well under control and succeed at what you want to happen. But, either in professional or personal relationships, you probably have found Learned Distress splattering all over the place. You may even feel powerless to make things feel good or go well in relation to other people.

Treadmill-Running Style: You have the best treadmill around, you tell everyone else what kind to buy or how to fix it, and you run masterfully. But you feel strong resistance if there's ever a need to listen to anyone else's guidance or leadership on running style, and you find it difficult to run in groups unless you can be coaching or winning. Any need to collaborate on running with someone else might fill you with dread, as the thought of having to work equally with someone else never seems to work out well for you.

Dictator SQ Pattern Breakdown

The rising intensity of the absolute insistence on your way as the only way is what overwhelms this survival mechanism's ability to persist. This causes clashes with other people in some or multiple parts of your life. A major way this happens is when you meet with a barrier to doing things your way, such as an authority figure or institutional structure, and you don't have the option of walking away. This might be because it's a societal structure that everyone has to work within or because the structure or authority figure holds the keys to your only pathway to doing something very important to you. One Dictator met his pattern's breaking point with the authorities and structures of graduate school because his career was so important to him that he couldn't walk away.

You might find your breaking point when working within groups. Your inability to listen to anyone else's point of view or to collaborate effectively gets in the way of accomplishing goals that are important to you. So, again, your Dictator pattern is pushed up against a wall.

Or that breaking point may come when people who are very important to you reject your way of doing things. They might even leave you for good, which leads you to see that this survival mechanism doesn't work for you anymore.

From Dictator to Well-Being

As layers of this Learned Distress pattern peel away, you can feel that you are able to relax and just be yourself. You might not have to show (or pretend) that you're perfect all the time or that you already know everything. One of my clients was shocked at herself when she was in a work meeting and these words flew out of her mouth: "I don't know." She couldn't believe no one died and the sky didn't fall!

You may be able to sit back and let others do things in their own way instead of reacting in your kneejerk way to jump in and tell them how. You might even find yourself listening to other people's viewpoints and even learn something—extra credit if you can admit you learned something! This can allow you to collaborate with others more easily, and you might find that you can be an integral part of a group, instead of only being in charge of it.

Finding yourself connecting with others in a more vulnerable way can be a new possibility. Maybe, for the first time, you feel connected to others just for being yourself and sharing what matters to you, rather than for telling them how to do something.

You may also find yourself able to work with organizational or societal structures in ways that work for you. That automatic impulse to oppose imposed rules calms down. You start to have space to evaluate what guidelines and structures might actually be *good* for you and others you care about, instead of rejecting them instantly.

One Dictator client saw these changes in both her professional and personal life. She'd started clashing with her mom early in life, and through her relationship with her mom, she could see that she

The (Benevolent) Dictator Pattern

always did one of two things: push back or get out. After her mom died, she still had challenges with a sister who had always closely aligned with her mom.

She went on a big vacation with this sister and, as often happens through Quanta Change, her newly uncovered well-being found a different way for her to relate and express herself than "push back or get out." She found she could say what she wanted to this sister, listen to what her sister had to say, and then step back and observe. She said, as clients often do to me, that she had a newfound space to observe and choose how to respond, instead of her usual reflexive responses. We hear so much about how we should be choosing the ways we respond to situations, but Learned Distress actually removes our ability to choose, while well-being can give us that space and ability to choose, not to mention the comfort with being ourselves that makes other people's opinions less threatening. The more we are okay being exactly who we are, the more we automatically allow others to be themselves.

In her professional life, she had worked for an organization in which she was being groomed for a leadership position in one division, which she had no interest in. When she turned down the leadership track, she was sent to a part of the organization where she said they thought the work would break her. She actually enjoyed it a lot more, but it's a great example of her "push back or get out" pattern. When she was doing Quanta Change, she was training for a new career, and the gatekeeper for that work was a dysfunctional leader who invited equally dysfunctional behavior in the program's students. My client, not surprisingly, not only clashed with the leader, she then was treated horribly by her fellow students and others in the organization. But, as she peeled off Learned Distress and felt more like she mattered for her own uniqueness, others in the broader organization invited her into a different training track, where she was honored and appreciated. Eventually, the students who had treated her badly actually apologized. Instead of having to walk away from this work that was so important to her, her well-being found another way forward, and she ended up having good relationships with even those who had been so negative toward her.

If you have the Dictator pattern, it truly is possible for you to be your genuine self, build healthy relationships, and put your intellect, capacity, and confidence to work for your own good and the good of others in ways that work more smoothly and easily than you've ever experienced.

CHAPTER 14

How to Overcome Common Obstacles and Bumps on Your Quanta Change Path

Did you recognize yourself in one or more of the six SQ patterns? Did you see behavior and emotional responses that you thought were uniquely miserable for you, but now understand that you're in good company? Were you even surprised to see that something you thought was a good trait of yours is something I'm saying is Learned Distress? Your survival mechanism may have allowed you to accomplish some pretty great things in your life. That is often the case, as it has been throughout history for many, and I celebrate all those successes. But what I have seen over and over, even in clients who have been tremendously accomplished in life, is that well-being can empower you to do so much more, more easily, and allow you to feel better while doing it. That is what I am looking forward to seeing you experience!

I hope you're excited to get your two-year-old sense of self moved over to the well-being road! But if your hope for feeling better is accompanied by any questions or hesitation, this chapter will address the most common obstacles that people face with the Quanta Change process.

Sleeping with the Sensory Message Recording

As a reminder, Element No. 2 of Quanta Change is sleeping with the specially designed recording that is the catalyst for removing layers of Learned Distress. There are a couple of concerns people express when we're first talking about their process related to playing this recording during sleep. I have never seen either of these concerns prevent someone from seeing robust, positive change.

The first is one I had at the beginning, too. I slept very poorly for years leading up to that point—for me, this was a few hours of sleep often followed by several hours awake worrying about *everything*, and then if I was lucky and had time, another couple or three hours asleep. I feared that if I couldn't sleep for eight hours through the night, this process couldn't work for me. And yet I saw big, positive changes start right away, the first of which was *better sleep*. (Yay!)

In fact, one frequent Quanta Change result in people who haven't slept well is better sleep fairly quickly. That's because Learned Distress stands in the way of good, effective sleep.

Learned Distress at its simplest level is the fear that there is something wrong with you. Fear triggers the stress response, a physiological reaction that releases hormones that allow you to fight, flee, or freeze—the fight or flight response. You are alert and ready to protect yourself, and you cannot be asleep and do that. When the trigger is something outside of you, say, a wild animal chasing you or a public speaking event, your stress response turns off after you successfully get through the event, and you can relax and go back to normal, including sleeping. But Learned Distress is fear trapped inside of you, and you can't get past it in the same way you would be able to stop responding to an external trigger. If your SQ pattern is one that allows you to feel lots of your Learned Distress all the time, you may see that negative impact in your sleep. But then, as you unlearn Learned Distress layers, the stress response automatically calms down, and you sleep better. (Again, yay!)

Another concern I hear regularly is from people who like or need silence to sleep, or from people who are afraid the recording will bother their significant other. There are several ways around this. One is to play the recording through earbuds or a pillow speaker that you put under your pillow. That way, only you will hear it. Another solution is to play the recording in another room. Now, I know, this seems weird, doesn't it? How are you going to get the benefit of the recording if you can't even hear it? The reality is that as long as the recording is playing in your home and there is at least some volume coming through the player, you will see the effects of the recording. You can play it at whatever volume and with whatever placement in your home works for you, I promise!

I have evidence of this both in my own houseguests and in family members of clients. One guest of mine who was sleeping two floors away from the recording said, "I don't know what it is about your house but I've never slept so well or had dreams like that in my life." Those are clear signs of response to the recording. And while adults have built up enough Learned Distress to make all three Quanta Change Elements necessary to see big change, children sometimes see significant change just from the recording playing. One client's children saw physical and emotional improvements that I could see were clearly a response to Quanta Change, but that the practitioners they had been seeing found to be amazing and even mysterious.

So, I hope this puts to rest any fears you might have about being able to play the recording while you sleep and have it work well for you.

Overcoming Natural Resistance to Change

Remember the wall of resistance to change and how it protects your survival mechanism from rational-level change? So, while it is true that Quanta Change gets around that wall by working with your brain during sleep, you might still experience the wall trying to manifest as you start your process. Here are some ways you might notice that happening.

Your resistance to change might show itself by interfering with you starting the process in some way. The most common version of this phenomenon is some temporary interference with the recording. I've seen it all over the past two decades! In the old days when I mailed CDs to clients, I had to send at least three to one person overseas before she finally received it. Another client's CD player just wouldn't open, despite the fact that she'd just changed a CD in it the day before! (This always reminds me of a baby who will *not* open their mouth for a spoonful of peas and it cracks me up to this day.) In the digital age, some clients have had trouble transferring the MP3 file to a phone, despite never having trouble doing that with any other file.

And then, all *kinds* of weirdness can happen by playing the recording. It will skip (even though MP3s shouldn't do that), your device will stop playing in the middle of the night, you will find that you keep turning it off overnight, and more. Listening to it can also get increasingly annoying for a short period. These bumps generally smooth out within a matter of days or a few weeks without any Herculean effort on your part.

You can also experience resistance to change that looks a lot like your SQ pattern—your survival mechanism can start talking loudly when you are preparing to burn layers of it off permanently. It's kind of understandable, right? But it may feel strange. Maybe like you're being pulled in two directions—your adult, rational brain saying, "Yes, I want to feel better and have my life work more easily *now*!" But, at the same time, feeling a familiar pull in the other direction. Here's how that might feel:

If you have the Idealist pattern, you might start to feel that you're just too busy for this right now, or you might start to think, "Really, everything is okay. Do I really need to do this right now? Probably not!"

If you have the Perfectionist pattern, it might feel scary or overwhelming to start the process. You might find ways in which this doesn't seem quite right for you or it seems too invasive. Or it might feel like it's *too much* in a way you can't quite pinpoint for yourself. You might even feel a little out of control.

If you have the Defeatist pattern, you have probably heard that voice of resistance jabbering at you the whole time you've been reading this book. "Sounds good, must be *nice* to get those results." (You know the script.) "But nothing ever works for you, so is there really even a point to trying this?" You might be thinking of a dozen reasons you can't start this right now, or you might also feel like that familiar force is just dragging you backward, even though you want to move forward into the process.

If you have the Caregiver pattern, you might actually be excited thinking about how much help and support you're going to get through this process. But there might be some way in which you feel like you can't do it, likely related to other people—maybe you can't find a Quanta Change session time (QC Element No. 1) when you can talk in private and without interruption because you have to cater to everyone else's needs first.

If you have the Optimist pattern, you might encounter a crisis in getting started. The good news for you is that you have the capacity to overcome that struggle, but if you're feeling "crisis fatigue," you might just have to push yourself through that to get going with Quanta Change. Or you might feel uneasy at the prospect of life working more easily for you.

If you have the Dictator pattern and you've read this far, you've already done a lot of overcoming! The biggest resistance to change in your pattern is listening to someone else's ideas about, well, anything. You might experience more of that familiar difficulty letting someone else's ideas and viewpoints influence your life in a big way. You might struggle with finding out stuff you didn't know about yourself because it's so uncomfortable to admit you don't know something.

No matter which pattern you have and in ways that are bigger than you might realize, you have probably felt that your survival mechanism is *who you are*—maybe *all* of who you are. Learned Distress can overwhelm your core well-being in such huge ways that your uniqueness, which is who you *truly* are, can be largely hidden from you. So, it can feel like you're just going to *disappear* if you burn off your survival mechanism. But that's just Learned Distress talking, and I promise that your well-being has much better things to say to you and many gifts to share with you. Pushing back against the resistance to change will be well worth it.

Navigating the Quanta Change Cycle

The Quanta Change Cycle was identified in Phase Three of the research, and it is the repeating cycle of change that shows us that Quanta Change is working. A cycle can last anywhere from a couple or three days to a bit longer than that. In each cycle, your brain excavates the most intense layer of Learned Distress for you at the moment so you can burn it off. This is what allows your natural well-being to expand and take its place so you feel better and life works better.

"Great!" you're thinking. "Let's get on with it. Why would you even be talking about such a thing in a chapter about obstacles?" Well, while this is indeed the forward movement of the process, parts of the cycle can be intense and feel lousy. What I really want you to hear right now is that your Quanta Change Guide is going to support you through every bit of it and celebrate with you when you reach the part of the cycle that feels great.

A particularly change-savvy client once said this right near the beginning of his Quanta Change process, and it was a perfect illustration of the excitement I feel for my clients when I see change cycle happening: "Sara, in the past week, our oven broke, our toddler spilled silver paint all over the living room carpet, and I had my first asthma attack in years. This stuff really works!" He got right away that the only way to get rid of Learned Distress is to feel it as it's headed out. Let me dive into the change cycle a little further.

The initial part of the change cycle will feel different, based on whether that Learned Distress has been at the surface or buried. If it's how you've been feeling for a long time (at-the-surface Learned Distress), you might just feel, "Same stuff, different day!" or it could feel slightly more intense than usual. If it's buried Learned Distress, you might be surprised or things might feel a little out of control because Learned Distress that has been hidden from you and under control is no longer either. One current client has a very literal physical experience of this—her face and head get really hot. She's not sick, and that feeling dissipates pretty quickly, but we've seen it so clearly tied to the change cycle that it's our sign that a big layer has surfaced for her. Other common experiences are intense negative memories coming up, emotional or situational turmoil, or even physical symptoms surfacing or ramping up.

Your brain then starts working to unlearn that layer during sleep, and there are two ways in which you might notice that. You might have a day here or there in which you feel sleepy or you might even wake up feeling exhausted—like you need a night of sleep to recover from your night of sleep! (Don't worry—this won't be constant or overwhelming.) Your sense of self recognizes that good work is taking place while you sleep, so it's saying, "Could you put me back to sleep so I can get more work done?" You might also become more aware of your dreams or your dreams might become more intense. Because dreams are the mechanism by which the sense of self recharges, they are also the vehicle for burning off Learned Distress, and we can see evidence of this furnace in action in the intensity of your dreams, as well as the images and narratives in them if you remember them.

(But you need not remember your dreams for Quanta Change to be working.)

Now, you've had some intense dreams, and you've permanently burned off a layer of Learned Distress. Awesome! Do you know what comes after burning a big log in a fireplace? You get the messy job of shoveling out the ashes!

In the change cycle, you experience this by a bit more of that feeling lousy. It's like that layer of Learned Distress is thumbing its nose at you on its final exit. *This bit rarely lasts for more than a day.* Sometimes, you'll feel confused, emotionally drained, sad, or angry. Sometimes, situations will be screwed up, like not being able to find your keys, get places on time, or get something important done that day.

And sometimes, Learned Distress can move out through your body by causing you to feel sick or in pain. This last one can sometimes last more than a day because Learned Distress tends to move a bit more slowly through physical matter—your body—than it does through your emotions. *Going through the change cycle is not a substitute for medical care,* so your Quanta Change Guide will always encourage you to continue seeking care from your doctor or other medical professionals while going through the process.

"Wait!" you're thinking, "That sounds a lot like my life right now! How is this any different from what I'm going through already?" Bear with me! Here's a different analogy that will help you understand why this part of the cycle looks like the parts of your life that feel awful, and why having a similar experience within the change cycle is good news.

Let's think about your sense of self as a tea kettle. It stores Learned Distress and well-being, remember? The water in the kettle is your Learned Distress. Time and experience do two things: they fill up the kettle (increasing intensity) and they turn up the heat. Sometimes, it gets hot enough to boil off some water, some Learned Distress. You have experienced this your whole life—it's when you've felt bad emotionally or mentally, have felt awful in a relationship or in your attempts to achieve goals, or you've been sick or in pain. *These have all just been ways for your sense of self to temporarily boil off a bit of that building Learned Distress.* Unfortunately, though, you then went to sleep having felt that Learned Distress intensely, your sense of self was recharged with it, and the tea kettle was filled up again.

Quanta Change actually turns up the heat a bit faster than normal, *so that you can boil off Learned Distress for good.* And, as a result, you see those same kinds of awful feeling experiences you've had before as the tea kettle is whistling like crazy. This is what we want to happen because now you're boiling off the Learned Distress permanently. The best news? *The air inside the tea kettle is your core well-being.* You're changing the balance of what is stored in your sense of self, moving the needle toward more and more well-being. And this is why you will receive hearty congratulations from your Quanta Change Guide for every epic tea-kettle-whistling day you've had. It's the evidence that some Learned Distress is really gone.

And you'll see the evidence right away. The next part of the change cycle is when you feel better in some way, and you didn't have to put in the effort you're used to expending to make that good feeling happen.

Here's an example from one of my clients. She was working on more openly revealing who she really is, and she had spontaneously started to share with friends and family on social media about a part of her story that had been very difficult and painful, the point in her life when a chronic illness forced monumental changes. She had a new Quanta Change shift question, which can really turn up the heat under the kettle, and did it ever! She had the biggest flare of her illness in a long time, as well as lots of painful memories flooding back in. She felt very disconnected, had difficulty communicating with a good friend, and it took her an entire week to write one paragraph for her social media posts. This part of the cycle included an anxiety-ridden dream about having to make a presentation for work when she only had half of it written. (Her brain chose a picture that represented for her the feeling of anxiety about *sharing herself through writing* in order to work on that piece of Learned Distress.) And then, once that layer (about not being able to communicate openly about who she is) boiled off, she found that writing her story flowed effortlessly. She wrote about what had been a very traumatic part of her story in just a few hours, made a couple of simple edits, and posted it. Not only is she telling her story openly for the first time, getting a lot of grateful responses from people who are learning more about her and her illness and feeling closer to her, but she's finding writing easier than it has ever been. This client's experience encapsulates both how intense a change cycle can be and what unprecedented change it can bring about.

This change cycle can be really intense, but your Quanta Change Guide will be there to support you every step of the way, and it will be worth it! You'll come to see that what you are experiencing is an upward spiral in which you get to keep feeling better each time you cycle around it.

CHAPTER 15

Conclusion: It's Time for You to Feel Good Just Being Yourself!

If I could have waved my magic wand while you read this book and instantly removed all of your Learned Distress and the pain and frustration that comes with it, I would have. But that would have required me to negate the physics that determines how your life works, and physics always seems to win. Bummer!

What I hope I've done, though, is given you a thorough picture of how Quanta Change works *with* physics—with your brain's natural recharging mechanism during sleep—to remove Learned Distress and uncover your natural well-being. I hope you're seeing that there really is a way to feel better and have a life that works more easily.

Quanta Change Boiled Down to Five Paragraphs

This view of being human and how life works can be a lot to take in. Maybe some of it was so different from what you've heard before that you feel a little overwhelmed. Sorry about that! But understanding this is all for the purpose of uncovering your well-being.

What covered your well-being up in the first place was the feeling you absorbed early in life that there's something wrong with you. This Learned Distress got trapped in your sense of self and kept growing in intensity over time, as your sleeping brain used the Learned Distress you experienced during the day to recharge your sense of self at night.

It's totally unfair, but your sense of self never grows up into a rational adult; it remains the two-year-old that stored Learned Distress as part of the way you survive and fit well in the world. Even more unfair, this sometimes-moody toddler is in the driver's seat of your life, taking you down a scenic well-being road or a bumpy Learned Distress road. That's because the equal and opposite reaction—the automatic work of energy—keeps generating moments straight out of your well-being or Learned Distress without your rational input or control. At best, your adult thinking self can find ways to cope with or temporarily manage the toddler's driving, but the growing intensity of Learned Distress causes it to veer onto bumpier roads over time, where you either feel worse or things in your life are going worse.

The Quanta Change Sensory Quotient defines which of the six SQ survival mechanism patterns outline the way you store Learned Distress and survive with it. What's great about the SQ is that you get to see that your negative stuff is not who you really are—it's just one (or more) of six boxes that your Learned Distress fits into. And you can unlearn Learned Distress! When you do, your unique well-being that doesn't fit into any boxes is increasingly freed up for you to enjoy and express in the world.

You might have felt like you keep running into a brick wall when you've tried methods of feeling better. That barrier is the wall of resistance to change, which is activated when your rational brain is operating. The Quanta Change research found a way to burst through that wall by engaging in the Three Integral Elements of this process—sharing with your Quanta Change Guide, sleeping with the Sensory Message recording, and shifting to a better feeling during your lousy moments. This combination brings about the kinds of unprecedented changes I've shared throughout the book.

My Wish for You

Remember my analogy about running on the treadmill to keep the light turned on? Really sit with it right now. Imagine how it feels to run constantly in order to produce everything you need. Maybe your treadmill breaks down sometimes, and you have to fix it (in the dark!). Or you're just *so tired* of running. Got a good feel for it?

Now, imagine yourself standing outside, letting the sunshine do all of that work for you. Imagine being freed up to thrive more and more of the time, instead of having to run as hard as you can just to survive.

And again, I'm not suggesting that you're going to sit around eating chocolate cake all day while living off the surprise inheritance from your long-lost millionaire aunt. Thriving means that you feel better and that you are supported by your well-being in a new way that enables you to express your uniqueness in the world joyfully.

You finally get to be yourself—seen, heard, and treated with kindness and respect in ways you've never experienced. You finally fit in the world, or maybe you feel that the world finally *welcomes you* to being just who you naturally are.

You either discover more of what you're here on the planet to do or if you already knew it, your pathway forward is clearer and easier. Being healthy gets easier, no matter how that has been for you to this point, so you're more able to enjoy your life and fulfill your unique purpose.

You look back to before you started Quanta Change, only able to recall in an intellectual way just how awful you felt, or how much you had to struggle for life to work, or how often you felt anxious, sad, or angry. You are really amazed at just how much better it feels to be you than it used to.

That is my wish for you.

Your Next Step to Feeling Better

Getting your free, personalized Sensory Quotient Report is the very next step toward moving your two-year-old driver over to the well-being road. Go to https://QuantaChange.com/SQ/ to take the test. I will personally graph your answers and prepare your report.

When I email your report to you, I will offer you a free 30-minute assessment phone call with me. Together, we'll take a look at the biggest challenge you're facing through the lens of your SQ pattern. I'll help you understand the connections and give you a sense of how Quanta Change typically unfolds when you remove that piece of Learned Distress. What I love most about having this SQ conversation is helping you see that Learned Distress really is the source of your biggest frustration and that you can unlearn it. And if you're ready, we can embark on uncovering and liberating your well-being through your Quanta Change process.

I look forward to hearing from you soon!

ABOUT THE AUTHOR

Sara Avery

Sara Avery, Quanta Change Executive Director, helps people permanently remove blocks to natural well-being in relationships, work life, health, daily life, and self-expression. After seeing profound, positive changes in her health and self-confidence in the first few months of her own Quanta Change, she knew this would be her life's work. For two decades, she has guided others through the process, drawing on a five-year collaboration with Quanta Change founder Mimi Herrmann. Her clients report unprecedented improvements, often after having tried many other avenues of healing and transformation.

For her first career as a professional violinist and violin teacher, she obtained degrees in violin performance from Wichita State University and the University of Michigan, and she was an Aspen Music Festival Violin Fellow. This career gave her deep insight into the great variety of ways we face fear and challenges, how we express ourselves in the world, how we relate to others in high-pressure situations, and how we learn.

She feels fortunate to live near Boulder, Colorado, where she can see the Rocky Mountains from her office window every day.

Acknowledgments

First, thank you to Quanta Change founder Mimi Herrmann, whom I was so fortunate to collaborate with and learn from, and whose work I am deeply grateful to be able to share every day. She always said that I was going to write a book, and while she passed on years ago, I imagine she is watching over me right now, saying, "Sweetyheart, you finally did it!"

Thank you to my English teacher and newspaper editor mom, Nancy Avery, for teaching me how to write and for showing me that women can do anything they want in the world.

Thank you to my dad, Howard Sparks, whose sense of humor I am told I inherited. That capacity for laughter has been invaluable in my work with clients and in communicating about these weighty topics.

Thank you to my photojournalist stepdad, John Avery, who taught me how to see and frame things and who took us on many adventures. Sharing this work in many forms has been a giant adventure of the best kind.

Acknowledgments

Thank you to everyone who has invited me into your lives as your Quanta Change Guide, revealed things that you've never told anyone, trusted me to walk with you as you unlearned your deepest pain, and allowed me to share in your joy at uncovering your well-being.

Thank you to my violin teachers, Julia Hoppes, Cecilia Shenold, Nancy Luttrell, Susan Linnebur, Andrzej Grabiec, Won-bin Yim, David Perry, and Paul Kantor, as well as my high school orchestra conductor, Steve Luttrell, from whom I learned how we learn, how to teach, how energy works, how applied physics works, and how differently and uniquely we can all express ourselves.

Thank you to the amazing wolf-dogs Sasha and Lexi for walking past my door so that I could connect with this work.

Thank you to Catherine Gregory, whose coaching and expertise made writing this book possible. Thank you to Catherine, Nathan Joblin and the entire Modern Wisdom Press team, whose collaboration brought this book into being.

Thank You

Dear reader, thank you so much for reading this book. I know that it may have stirred up a lot for you, but I hope it has answered some questions and, most of all, given you hope! If you haven't already, please take advantage of the free Sensory Quotient test on my website: www.QuantaChange.com/SQ and sign up for the free 30-minute call that I offer when I send your personalized SQ report.

If you found this book helpful, I hope you will also take a few minutes to review it on Amazon.

Thanks, once again, and I look forward to hearing from you soon!

www.ingramcontent.com/pod-product-compliance
Lightning Source LLC
Chambersburg PA
CBHW021954290426
44108CB00012B/1066